LAW AND LOVE

LAW AND LOVE

by Helen Oppenheimer

A STUDY IN PRACTICAL CHRISTIAN ETHICS

With a Foreword by Canon G. B. Bentley

THE FAITH PRESS

7 TUFTON STREET LONDON S.W.I

PRINTED IN GREAT BRITAIN
in 10 point Garamond type
BY THE FAITH PRESS LTD
LEIGHTON BUZZARD

TO M.B.G.O.

FOREWORD

THERE are a great many professing Christians who will tell you that Christianity consists in 'living a good life'. If you try to discover what they mean by this, you will probably bring to light a curious state of affairs : on the one hand it will appear that a man is called 'good-living' if he measures up to the code—often a not very exalted code—of the social group to which your informant belongs; on the other it will be insisted that the standard of goodness is 'the teaching of Christ', particularly the Sermon on the Mount. What is odd about this is that usually it is hard to find a single saying in the 'Sermon on the Mount' that is in fact endorsed by the code in question.

Yet there is no reason to doubt the sincerity of those who claim the authority of Christ's teaching for their moral attitudes. Rather it seems that very few people indeed manage to see what is actually written in the Gospels : the majority look at the teaching through tinted spectacles of one shade or another and only find in it a reflection of the codes in which they were brought up.

It is therefore no trivial service that Lady Oppenheimer does us when she makes us discard our spectacles and see what Christ in fact said. The immediate result of this confrontation is, as always, bewilderment. We feel afresh the tremendous impact of the teaching : our consciences are sensibly pricked; and yet—to come down to brass tacks—what does it all mean in terms of behaviour? Here, apparently, are definite moral precepts of patent authority; but they just will not combine with the commonsense morality of justice and rights and duties by which we believe ourselves bound. If we attempt to sew them on to the fabric of that morality, the new cloth only pulls away from the old and tears it.

So what are we to do? With the various devices for taking the edge off Christ's teaching Lady Oppenheimer will have nothing to do. She insists that Christ gave us definite precepts—not optional 'counsels', nor so-called 'principles', nor even impossible yet relevant 'ideals'. But (she maintains) we shall never make sense of these precepts if we try to treat them as a more rigorous and demanding expression of the morality of rights and duties. To follow Christ we have to *transcend* that morality; for 'Christian morals are a way, not a code : the Christian spirit does not consist in keeping the rules better than other people nor in keeping stricter rules, but in going beyond rules altogether'.

But how can we 'transcend' rights and duties? Quite simply. We can transcend them by behaving as people commonly do behave in family life : that is, by responding to the demands, not of moral rules, but of personal relationships. In family life rights and duties are not indeed abolished, nor are rules without a place, but all those things are subsumed by family love. The teaching of Christ is that this morality of personal relationships can and should be extended beyond the natural family to embrace the whole family of the children of God.

Put baldly like this Lady Oppenheimer's thesis may not sound strikingly original. After all we have heard before that the law is only a school-master to bring us to Christ and that in Christ we are not under law but under grace. But the value and attraction of this book lie in the masterly and persuasive simplicity with which the model of family life is used to illuminate facet after facet of the Gospel and to lay bare the complexities of the human heart. Moreover it is an absorbing—one could almost say an exciting—book to read; and that, seeing how dull a topic morals can be, is an achievement of no mean order.

I do not say that I am equally convinced by every application of the model. For instance, although I am sure it is right to apply it to Church discipline, where it provides an antidote to the legalistic thinking that goes with the notion of *societas perfecta,* the discussion of church-going and of divorce and remarriage, stimulating as it is, leaves me wondering whether it is possible to consider these questions in terms of Christian *morals* alone.

I agree that, so far as public worship is meant to be an expression of one's family relationship to God and one's fellow Christians, an imposed rule about church-going is of little avail, since it cannot secure anything more than 'the external fact of attendance'. But is there not another factor that needs to be considered? The Eucharist is not only the *expression* of Christian family love, but also the sacramental *source* of that love, and indeed a constitutive principle of the family, which cannot exist apart from it. But if that is so, does not 'the external fact of attendance' become itself an end that must be attained? Unless the family can be brought to the family Table there is no possibility of the family relationships being realized.

And then divorce and remarriage. I am personally grateful to Lady Oppenheimer for the reminder (which I needed) that one of Christ's sayings about divorce occurs in the Sermon on the Mount. Its context suggests that 'Whosoever shall marry her that is divorced committeth adultery' is the same order as the description of lust as adultery and the warnings against anger and retaliation, and that like them it transcends rights and duties. Now the Church does not think it appropriate to make disciplinary laws about the other offences against family love—angry words, lustful thoughts and the vindication of rights; why then should it do so in the case of divorce and remarriage?

I believe there is something true and important to be learned from this about the moral aspect of the relationship between husband and wife and about the attitude the family of Christians should take towards husbands and wives who fall short in love. But does not the question again arise whether it is enough to consider the *moral* aspect? Is there not also an *ontological* aspect to notice? What Christ said about marriage elsewhere suggests that there is; and there is confirmation in the fact that it makes sense to ask about a marriage after divorce, or indeed about any putative marriage, whether it is 'really' a marriage—and that quite independently of any judgment on the moral condition of the parties.

To put this *caveat* in another way, it seems to me that it is peculiarly difficult to apply the model of family love to the situation of the family of Christians when it is faced by divorce and remarriage among its members. And the reason seems to be this. Family love is able to take in its stride all sorts of offences against love; but if the father of the family decisively repudiates the mother by marrying someone else, he does more than offend against love : he destroys the fundamental unity on which the very existence of the family depends.

But I must not let this develop into a review. What I have written will, I hope, show that this book has given me a great deal to think about. I feel sure that other readers will have a like experience.

The Cloisters, Windsor Castle.   G. B. BENTLEY
November 14th, 1961

PREFACE

THIS book and particularly Chapter 8 grew out of an article which appeared in *Theology* (August 1957) and I am grateful to the Editor and to the Director of the S.P.C.K. for permission to make use of what I wrote there.

I should like to thank all the people who have helped me, especially Miss K. M. Lea, Professor Dorothy Emmet, Mrs. W. Kneale, the Revd. Gordon Hewitt and Mrs. Hewitt, for their kind interest and valuable comments upon this book or the *Theology* article. My special thanks are due to my husband and to the Revd. D. D. Evans, both of whom have read practically the whole book as it was written and made innumerable helpful criticisms both of style and sense. Naturally none of these is responsible for any opinions I have expressed or any errors I have made.

In quoting from the Bible I have generally used the American Revised Standard Version. Sometimes I have used the New English Bible and indicated this in the footnotes. I should have liked to have made more use of it, but its renderings are still too unfamiliar to make their effect in short quotations.

L.H.O.

CONTENTS

CHAPTER 1

Strictness and Kindness

THE function of the Church is to witness to the Gospel, but it cannot be denied that at the present time its witness is sometimes extremely blurred, and that a basic reason for this is Christian disunity. The problem with which I am concerned is a problem of Christian disunity: not the conspicuous and indeed notorious separation of the Christian communions from one another, but a conflict that is almost as fundamental although it does not exactly follow denominational lines.

This conflict is about the nature of Christian morality itself, and it is seriously reducing the effectiveness of all Christian teaching. Churchmen tend to take one of two attitudes, each of which can be stated most convincingly and for each of which they can claim the authority of Christ. One of these attitudes is an uncompromising insistence on principle which will not water down Christian teaching even for the sake of hard cases; the other is a general benevolence which makes kindness the only real Christian virtue.

On the one hand it may be pointed out that since the Gospel is the most precious thing we have it is of overriding importance that it should in no way be compromised. Christ said that it is better to cut off hand or foot or eye if it is hindering one from entering the kingdom of God,[1] and that a disciple of his must be willing to reject 'father and mother and wife and children and brothers and sisters, yes, and even his own life.'[2] No one, he said, 'who puts his hand to the plough and looks back is fit for the kingdom of God.'[3] Once, it may be pointed out, Christians were willing to die for their faith, and if they had not been the Church could never have survived: then surely the least we can do is take Christianity seriously in our lives and pass it on intact to the next generation. If Christ said something we must believe that he meant it. It is true that he often spoke metaphorically; we are not literally to cut off our feet or carry a cross, but we ought to be willing

---

[1] Mark 9: 43–7.
[2] This is put at its strongest in Luke 14: 26. Canon Lindsay Dewar explains that ' "to hate" is a Hebraic way of expressing "to love less than" ' (*An Outline of New Testament Ethics*, p. 91).
[3] Luke 9: 62.

to be no less heroic. It is the duty of the Church to uphold Christ's standards however difficult this may be, even at the cost of appearing narrow, churlish or fanatical. The martyrs must have appeared to be all these things; but Christ warned his followers that they would be hated by all for his name's sake,[4] and that he did not come to bring peace but a sword.[5]

The opposite point of view is no less convincing. It insists that the most characteristic Christian message is of love and forgiveness for all men, and that just as Christ went about doing good, so we ought above all to try to imitate his kindness. 'Him who comes to me I will not cast out,' [6] he said; and he consorted with outcasts and was ready to offend against some of the most cherished principles of the religious men of his day. He 'came not to call the righteous, but sinners.' [7] Likewise we must have flexible minds, not be easily shocked, and be willing to find goodness in unlikely places rather than look for merely conventional righteousness. We are not to judge others,[8] but follow Christ's example of love.

None the less, although each of these attitudes is very convincing in itself, they are both doing harm in the Church to-day, and both are bringing Christianity into disrepute. The first, the uncompromising attitude, drives many people out of the Church. One hears far too often of people who would gladly call themselves Christians, who teach their children to say their prayers and who try to set them a good example, who are energetic and useful as members of the community, but who simply cannot see the relevance of the Church as it is to-day to the teaching of Christ in the New Testament. Sometimes they have never really been in touch with the Church, but have disliked what they have heard of it. Sometimes they have approached it, perhaps over a question of a child's baptism or a wedding, and have been rebuffed for some reason. Sometimes they have been churchgoers but have come into conflict with their vicar over some matter of principle. He thinks them lax, they think him bigoted, and neither really understands the other's point of view. Whatever the actual reason, harm out of all proportion is done to the Church.

This is not only a matter of empty pews. People see their friends

[4] Matthew 10: 22; cf. John 15: 19.
[5] Matthew 10: 34.
[6] John 6: 37.
[7] Matthew 9: 13.
[8] Matthew 7: 1.

whom they like and trust living in estrangement from the Church, and their own religion, if they have any, is weakened; or if they have none they are less likely to feel the need for any. This kind of example is far more dangerous than what is usually called a 'bad example.' Not many people are tempted to imitate open and notorious evil livers, but most are tempted to fit in with those around them. When those around them are obviously decent good people who have been alienated by the apparently unsympathetic treatment they have received from the Church, it is the Church that comes into disrepute. Non-Christians are quick to point out that Christ himself said, 'Judge not,' and as quick to notice when his followers do not live up to his teaching. The result is that instead of his disciples being recognized, as he wished, by their love for one another,[9] we are faced by the bitter irony of the converse coming true: people cannot believe that the Church is the Body of Christ when its members seem to have so little love or understanding that they are even willing to drive one another out of the Christian fellowship.

It may be said that the Church does not want to fill its pews with merely nominal Christians, and that if by tightening its requirements and insisting on quality rather than quantity it can show who are its loyal members, so much the better. But this will not do. The Church is not meant to be a clique of virtuous people perfecting their own salvation: it is one of its primary duties to go after the lost sheep. It cannot merely insist on its principles and let people take it or leave it; it ought to look on vague religion as a basis to build on, not just a form of idleness to scorn.

The opposite point of view, which exalts kindness above everything, does just as much harm. Many people, brought up on the idea of 'gentle Jesus, meek and mild,' with all the sternness in the New Testament left out, never come to feel that religion is anything which requires them to take any trouble. It is a beautiful story for children, a spiritual background at Christmas when everything else is so secular and commercial, a charming picturesque feature of foreign countries and perhaps a bulwark against Communism; but not something which one would actually take into account when making some difficult decision, or something which could alter one's daily life. People have been taught that God forgives, but not about the cost of forgiveness, and they simply assume that God will 'understand' if they live self-

[9] John 13: 35.

indulgent lives and never come to Church. 'Dieu me pardonnera : c'est son métier' is an attitude which is often taken up in no spirit of cynicism.

The prevalence of this attitude can do just as much harm outside the Church as one of unyielding insistence on principle. People cannot respect a Church which never makes a moral stand, and are much less likely to come to worship a God who seems to make no real demands on them. Tolerance and kindness are a good deal, but they are not everything; and it is not possible to base a satisfactory religion on them alone.

In these circumstances it is hardly possible for the Gospel to come as Good News. On the one hand there are many people, especially those who have had a strict upbringing, to whom it is simply bad news : Christianity is something which stops you doing what you want. Instead of a Gospel we then have a religion of fear which sets out to restrict all kinds of pleasure as much as possible and which teaches that God is a God of punishment. This may sound like a caricature; but it is a caricature which is too often accepted as a true picture both by Christians and non-Christians. The result is either a very one-sided religion or an understandable hostility to any religion at all.

But probably still more prevalent is the opposite attitude which makes religion into a sort of optional extra and has no need for a Gospel. It does not require the Incarnation of the Son of God to tell us that we ought to be kind to each other; many purely human teachers have had more inspiring messages than that. It is only if we are conscious of being sinners in need of redemption that Christianity is really Good News.

It is not possible to make a satisfactory compromise between these two attitudes. It will not do to be moderately strict and yet moderately kind. Each makes an absolute demand, and we are told to be perfect. We are to make no compromise with evil, and yet we are to have limitless charity to all men. Neither of these is to be watered down.

Nor is it possible to reconcile them in a simple way by saying that we must adopt the strict attitude for ourselves and the kind one for other people. It is not at all desirable to try to hold two standards at once. One cannot be entirely blind to other people's behaviour; yet to maintain that it is all right for them to behave badly but not for oneself leads to either mental dishonesty or pride. It is not even safe to assume that either of the two attitudes, strictness to oneself and kindness to others, is invariably satisfactory in itself. It can be very harmful to be merciless to oneself and forget that Christianity should be a joyful religion. On the other hand it is not always desirable to show unlimited tolerance to others : people can often help one another by strictness. A man may be inspired by a difficult challenge or brought to his senses by a sudden chance to see himself as others see him. Although we are told not to judge, this does not mean that we have no responsibilities; and it is difficult, both in theory and practice, to distinguish 'not judging' from condoning evil. If we refuse to show disapproval of something we think bad we may seem to encourage it.

It is fashionable nowadays when faced with this sort of question to speak of a 'tension' in Christianity between two opposite poles, in this case strictness and kindness. This there clearly is; but to say so merely states and does not solve the problem. I am not suggesting that the tension cannot be resolved. There are people who seem to find the answer instinctively, who combine unselfconsciously the highest integrity with the most profound kindliness and charity. But this is no general answer. It is no help to the ordinary person simply to be told to 'be a saint.' One needs more specific guidance. It may be objected that to 'be a saint' is just what we are told : 'You, therefore, must be perfect, as your heavenly Father is perfect' [10]; but this is no isolated commandment which we are expected to understand and obey on its own. It comes as a summary and climax of a long series of detailed commands. The trouble is that to-day we do not seem to find their right interpretation self-evident.

---

[10] Matthew 5 : 48.

CHAPTER 2

Rigorism and Rules

SINCE it is the New Testament teaching itself, with its two aspects of sternness and gentleness, which sets the problem, it is necessary to look at this teaching and try to discover the most Christian answer. But a preliminary objection may be raised : is this a reasonable procedure? It may well be asked whether we have a sufficiently reliable record of what Christ's words were, and by what right we take his precepts as authoritative. Non-Christians want to know why any sensible person should accept as categorical commands the teaching of someone, however good, who lived nearly two thousand years ago. They feel, not unreasonably, that it would be much better to weigh the facts as they are in the modern world and try to maximize happiness. They do not look on the teaching of Christ as basic but simply an extra fact, the advice of one wise man, which might easily be bettered by the most competent modern sociologists.

Clearly this is not the place to embark on elaborate apologetics. All I can do is make my assumptions explicit and hope that they will then not appear wholly arbitrary. I am assuming that the close historical scrutiny which has been applied to the New Testament records for many years now has not been able to discredit their general reliability nor eliminate their supernatural aspect. To some people the supernatural as such is incredible; but if the possibility of the supernatural is allowed, the New Testament books, after much stringent testing, have a strong claim to be accepted as sound historical sources, giving a reliable account of Christ's words and actions.[1]

Secondly, I am assuming that an integral part of these sources is their claim that Jesus Christ is God Incarnate. Here I would put particular weight on the fact that he preached repentance yet showed no sense of sin, and indeed claimed to forgive other people's sins. His contemporaries saw the point, and accused him of blasphemy.[2] If his claim is not blasphemy nor illusion his teaching is authoritative. The alternative is to reject the Christian Gospel in its entirety. These argu-

[1] See e.g. C. H. Dodd, *History and the Gospel*; Vincent Taylor, *The Gospels*; Richard Heard, *An Introduction to the New Testament*.
[2] e.g. Mark 2 : 7.

16

ments do not give us the right to build too much on any isolated text, for it is not inerrancy which is claimed, only general soundness; but on the other hand we certainly have no right to reject any particular piece of teaching which happens to be inconvenient for our way of thinking, unless there are good independent reasons for so doing.

If we accept the authority of Christ we cannot hold that he was merely a wise moral teacher with whom we may disagree. Nor on the other hand can we hold that he was not setting forth a permanent system of morals at all. To some scholars it seems very probable that during his earthly life Jesus Christ expected the end of the world to come at once.[3] Without attempting detailed criticisms of this view we can see that if his whole doctrine was based on such an expectation then the foundations of our modern Christianity become extremely shaky. If Christ's teaching was expressly intended as an 'interim ethic,' a heroic way of life for a brief time of crisis, it is hard to see what relevance it is supposed to have for us nearly two thousand years later.

If, taking the Gospels as a whole, one believes on the contrary that Christian ethics have and were meant to have a permanent validity the critical problem at once arises of how they are to be interpreted. Unfortunately this problem is by no means easy. Even the 'Sermon on the Mount,' to which the most nominal of Christians pays lip-service, is full of precepts which nowadays good men daily repudiate or try to tone down in the name of morality itself. We think of it as the highest and most inspiring teaching mankind has ever received; yet when we come to apply it to ourselves or still more to others we run into grave difficulties, not only because we cannot keep it, but because sometimes we are not even sure that we ought to keep it. For example, Christ said, 'Whoever marries a divorced woman commits adultery'[4] : but we do not believe that someone who has remarried after divorce is on exactly the same footing as someone who is openly living in sin. Christ said, 'Do not resist one who is evil. But if any one strikes you on the right cheek, turn to him the other also; and if any one would sue you and take your coat, let him have your cloak as well'[5] : but we are sure that justice ought to be done and that we ought not always to submit to violence or hand over our property to others on demand. Christ said, 'Give to him who begs from you, and do not refuse him who would

---

[3] e.g. Schweitzer, *The Quest of the Historical Jesus*, p. 352.
[4] Matthew 5: 32.
[5] Matthew 5: 39–40.

17

B

borrow from you' [6] : but we do not want to encourage other people in bad ways. These are only a few examples of teaching which people to-day are apt to feel is harsh, unrealistic or even wrong. Plenty of other examples might be given from all the Gospels. If we take Christ's teaching at its face value as a rule of life we have great difficulty in applying it in practice; and yet if we take it at anything less than its face value we cannot help feeling that this is a kind of betrayal.

I shall try to show that the problem is not insoluble, and that Christian morals rightly understood are impressively realistic and coherent; but the problem cannot be solved by over-simplification, nor by picking out the parts of the New Testament which we happen to like best. If we accept the Christian Gospel at all it is our duty to take full account of every strand of thought which is to be found in it.

Many people feel compelled to adopt a strict interpretation of all Christ's words and try to apply them as rules of life, facing their implications and consequences with honesty. This is Rigorism; and it is a position which deserves respect. If it were merely difficult to keep Christ's commandments it would be our clear duty as loyal Christians to adopt this view, admit no exceptions, and hope for grace to enable us to do what we cannot do by nature. The real problem is when Rigorism is not only hard but seems to lead to conclusions which go against our consciences quite as much as against our inclinations, which lead us at times into impossible situations,[7] and which are not even in the end compatible with the teaching of Christ.

The Rigorist will reply that the reason why Christian teaching when taken strictly offends our modern conscience is that our modern conscience is corrupt. It is the plain fact, he will point out, that Christ told us to do and not to do certain things, and we ignore this at our peril. He can therefore argue persuasively that we ought to have the courage to stand firm, do as we are told, and leave the issue in God's hands. This is heroic, but it will not do. It is a counsel of despair to say that our consciences are corrupt. The same consciences tell us to follow Christ : if we cannot trust them we are left, not with Christianity, but with complete scepticism about how we are to find out what our duty is.

The Rigorist however assumes that our consciences are inspired by the Holy Spirit in telling us to obey Christ, however wrong they may

[6] Matthew 5 : 42.
[7] See e.g. Chapter 8.

be over particular moral questions. He therefore tries with courage and integrity to put this conviction into practice; but the difficulties are greater than he supposes, for he finds himself obliged to be not only stern but also legalistic. He is frequently obliged to try to decide moral questions by niceties of interpretation of Christ's words. He must apply to the textual critic rather than the saint to find out what is the will of God for people to-day. This seems completely out of keeping with Christ's own way : he was unsympathetic to legalism,[8] refused to give legal answers to his questioners,[9] and attached far more importance to humility and repentance than to moral strictness.[10] Since he was no Rigorist himself,[11] and more particularly since he opposed those who took up this attitude in his day,[12] it is hard to believe that he really meant his followers to become Rigorists about his teaching.

I believe not only that Rigorism fails to supply a satisfactory interpretation of Christian morals, but that this failure is inevitable because Rigorism is based on a fundamental error. There is an inherent contradiction in trying to achieve holiness by means of a system of rules. It is not a question of the adequacy or inadequacy of any particular set of rules; it is the whole conception of holiness as the same kind of thing as legality which is unsatisfactory. Almost every one agrees that Acts of Parliament cannot make people good; but it is not so often recognized, although I hope to show that it is just the same principle, that rules of life cannot make people saints.

The man who sets out to be a saint by keeping to a rule of life is not the typical Christian but the typical Pharisee. He has a noble aim and may be deeply sincere, but he is on the wrong lines. It was no accident that the Pharisees came into conflict with Christ. It was not that they simply happened to be a bad or hypocritical group of people : it is widely agreed that in fact many of them were admirable; but they were basing their lives on a mistaken, and dangerously mistaken, theory. Keeping rules for the good of one's soul is a kind of self-discipline; but practising self-discipline for the sake of spiritual advancement is

---

[8] e.g. Mark 3 : 1–6; 7 : 1–23; Matthew 23 : 16–22.
[9] e.g. Luke 12 : 13–15.
[10] e.g. Matthew 9 : 13; 18 : 12–13; Luke 7 : 47; 15 : 11–32; 18 : 9–14; 23 : 43.
[11] It would be dishonest to deny that here and there, especially in the Gospel according to St. Matthew, we can find a few apparently Rigorist texts (e.g. Matthew 5 : 17–20; 23 : 1–3); but to try to build up a picture of a Rigorist Christ from these is to go against the whole impression given by the New Testament in general.
[12] e.g. Luke 11 : 46.

not a way of becoming 'unselfish,' any more than practising self-discipline for the sake of secular advancement is. Spiritual ambition may even turn out to be further from real goodness than ordinary ambition, for it is essentially self-regarding. A man may give up smoking in order to be a good athlete, or work long hours for the sake of political success, and although there is nothing specially moral about this at least his energies are directed towards something outside himself; whereas a man who adopts a rule of life for the sake of his own spiritual welfare is turned in on himself.

This can most easily be seen in the extreme case. Someone who puts his own principles before his love or consideration for other people can often be more wicked than someone who is straightforwardly self-indulgent without considering moral issues at all. We find it much easier to forgive a warm-hearted sinner than a persecutor, a bigot or a prig, and the Gospels give us excellent authority for this preference.

The problem is by no means confined to the extreme case. It arises very simply. If a man is rather bad and would like to be better the first step he is told to take is to keep the basic rules of morality, tell the truth, act fairly, and not be quarrelsome or sensual. So far, so good; but at the next stage the trouble begins. It is easy to say that in order to be better still he must keep stricter rules, fast and pray and deny himself, read holy books and do works of charity. The Christian Gospel is often taken as a message of this kind. It is supposed to be the new law of God leading us on to higher things, the special standard we must reach in order to attain to the Kingdom of Heaven; but when it is presented in these terms it leads straight into a dilemma.

If one has undertaken the obeying of a law in order to be good neither failure nor success is satisfactory. Failure to keep it must eventually lead, humanly speaking, either to despair or to a lowering of standards. Either one cannot bear one's failure, or one can bear it too well. Success on the other hand confronts one with the two alternatives, either that this is a creditable achievement, or that the law was not strict enough; and both these have most unsatisfactory consequences.

The sense of moral achievement leads straight to spiritual pride. It is hardly possible to avoid comparing oneself with other people who have succeeded less well, and then honesty of mind can only be maintained at the cost of humility. One cannot deny having kept the rules, nor pretend that this was just a private whim of one's own rather than a duty. All one can do is 'make allowances' for the other people, and this is hardly a humble activity. 'Of course,' one may say, 'it is up to me to go to Communion regularly in obedience to Christ's word, but it is not for me to worry if X hardly ever goes. He is at least a Christian and tries to love his neighbour. Y seems to have no standards at all; but I am not to blame him either : it must be his upbringing.' This sort of thing is uncomfortably close to the Pharisee's prayer : 'God, I thank thee that I am not like other men, extortioners, unjust, adulterers, or even like this tax collector.' [13] Perhaps a true Christian ought not to notice that other people do not always keep up as high a standard as himself; but if his own high standard is the result of having consciously set himself to obey a rule of life he can hardly help noticing, as the rule keeps drawing his attention to the question of success or failure. Wilful blindness is certainly not a Christian virtue, and once the problem has presented itself in these terms it is too late to go back to an earlier stage of unselfconsciousness.

This means that keeping moral rules successfully can be dangerous rather than beneficial. Spiritual pride is extremely insidious, for it does not present itself as a temptation like other sins : it is like a trap which a person with the best possible intentions can walk into unawares. The difficulty can start even in childhood. Children often have a very strong wish to be good, and it is natural to think that this can best be achieved by keeping all the rules and never being naughty. But grown-up people, including those in authority, are inclined to look on a child like this as a 'horrid little prig,' lacking something that is a proper feature of healthy childhood. They would positively prefer the child to be naughty sometimes, and this is a perfectly legitimate feeling. It does not come from jealousy or lack of appreciation of real good-ness, but from realizing that priggishness is not the same thing as holiness.

In a similar way, therefore, one cannot help wondering if this might be how God sees some of His would-be zealous servants. Yet to advocate the deliberate breaking of a suitably chosen selection of rules for one's soul's health is either cynicism or nonsense. Nor is it any use simply to tell people to forget themselves and think of others instead : for-getting oneself is not a thing which can be done to order; and thinking of others can easily in its turn be made into a rule to think of others for the good of one's own soul, so that one is back in the same predica-

13 Luke 18 : 11.

ment of self-centredness. He that would save his soul, one might almost say, shall lose it.

Alternatively, if a person has kept the rules he may conclude, not that he is virtuous, but that the rules were not strict enough or that he has interpreted them too leniently. Unfortunately this is just as harmful as consciousness of achievement, for it leads to a vicious regress, the name of which is scrupulosity. Once one starts asking whether one's rule of life is strict enough the answer is almost bound to be No. There seems no limit to this : a Christian dare not claim any rights at all. Yet the sternest self-discipline undertaken in this way need not be any help towards real goodness, and can even become a way not of curing one's sins but of making small sins into big ones. For example, a man knows he is greedy, and resolves to overcome it. If he tries to do this by setting himself a rule he is likely to find that he is as greedy as ever and perhaps more so, for his greed does not lie in the actual amount of food he eats but in his attitude to it. The attempt to decide how much or little to allow himself focusses his attention upon the question of his own gastronomic satisfaction in just the way he really wants to avoid. No rule, however strict, will be strict enough, for no rule can free him from self-concern; and here again it is too late to go back to the stage of innocent unselfconscious enjoyment.

The extreme case and indeed the *reductio ad absurdum* of the attempt to be good by setting oneself rules is self-regarding asceticism. The wish to deny oneself can in some people become exceedingly strong, and if it is given full rein it is not a wholesome tendency. It is possible to 'make a martyr' of oneself without being a saint : 'If I give away all I have, and if I deliver my body to be burned, but not have love, I gain nothing.' [14] An independent hermit practising self-mortification on his own, or worse still in competition with others, runs a risk of injuring not only his bodily but his mental health instead of achieving holiness.

Here the Rigorist may point out that the historic answer to this problem was monasticism. A monastic Rule does not only maintain a certain standard of discipline and make an ascetic way of life compulsory : it is explicitly designed as a way of preventing scrupulosity. In a religious community a man has a chance to forget himself, for his rule of life is set by someone else and it is not for him to worry about whether it is strict enough. The Rule has become an objective standard

[14] I Corinthians 13 : 3.

which it is his straightforward duty to obey, and provides the framework in which all the positive aims of monasticism are set. It is one way for people to become as little children in order to enter the Kingdom of God.

Of course it is only one way. Very few people have a vocation to leave the world and become monks or nuns : the great majority neither can nor should. On the other hand the Rigorist may point out that not many people have an acute temptation to scrupulosity. He may plausibly suggest that just as monasticism is the answer to the extreme, so a milder but corresponding answer is to be found for the milder but much more usual case.

He may therefore argue that it is the duty of the Church to set the rules for all her children, to put before them clearly what God requires of them in everyday life, so that they know what they ought to do and need not worry about whether they have done enough or become proud competing with one another. A good deal can be said on behalf of this kind of system. It need not be harsh or burdensome : to many people a regular, obedient way of life is positively joyful. The pious Jew delights in the law of God : 'Thy word is a lamp to my feet and a light to my path . . . Thy testimonies are my heritage for ever, yea, they are the joy of my heart.' [15] The good Catholic has no need to eat his fish on Friday with a long face; and in going to Mass every Sunday he is not only obedient but happy. A system like this can allow for feasts and fasts, for special occasions and for unusual circumstances, and can give to those who follow it a great sense of security and of being looked after.

All this is true, but it does not prove nearly as much as the Rigorist might think. What it means is that a system of rules can be animated by a genuine spirit of love; but this in no way shows that living by rules as such can make people good. Rules can be kept mechanically or reluctantly, for fear of the consequences or for the sake of a reward; to say that someone has kept a rule tells us nothing about the spirit in which he acted, and as soon as we inquire about the spirit we admit that the rule alone, however good as a rule, is not enough. Even Christian principles cannot by themselves make us into Christian people. For example, considered as a rule, and acted on without love, the precept 'If any one would sue you and take your coat, let him have

---

[15] Psalm 119 : 105, 111.

your cloak as well' [16] need be no more Christian than 'an eye for an eye, and a tooth for a tooth.' There is no merit in simply being unfair to oneself : it may be more cold-hearted than being fair. The spirit of bitterness and hate can be even stronger when it is allowed no outlet, and the secret feeling that one has let oneself be wronged leads to self-righteousness, not to love of one's enemies. Where a system of rules works at its best and people find peace and happiness under it this means that the rules are acting as a useful framework within which the spirit of love has a chance to operate. It does not mean that the rules themselves can be relied on to bring about any real goodness at all.

In practice most people recognize this. Moralists are always warning one of the dangers of formalism; and as soon as someone succeeds in evading the spirit of a rule while keeping closely to the letter everyone realizes what has gone wrong. The good Christian does not think a great deal about his duty; he is not constantly asking permission to do things or working out that seventy times seven is four hundred and ninety.[17] It is easy to see that morality does not consist in keeping rules mechanically, but it is not so often realized that rules, by definition, are essentially only 'the letter,' and that therefore 'the spirit,' which is what really counts, must inevitably be something over and above any form of rule.

One may put this in a different way by saying that goodness is not a standard. If a man is trying to keep rules, whether he has succeeded or not is an objective fact. The standard may be exceedingly high, but if the rules are explicit there still comes a point at which it has definitely been achieved, and he can say that he has kept the rules, that he is 'as to righteousness under the law blameless.' [18] But goodness is not like this : to stop, at whatever point, is to fall short. One can sometimes say 'Now I am law-abiding,' but as soon as someone says 'Now I am good' he has ceased to be so.

Nobody therefore can ever safely trust his whole moral life to any system of rules, for if he does he is leaving out the most important thing; and no Church can ever say, 'Keep these rules and you will be all right,' however carefully formulated, complete and flexible the rules may be. To ask, 'How can I be morally safe?' is really no more

[16] Matthew 5 : 40.
[17] Matthew 18 : 22.
[18] Philippians 3 : 6.

Christian than to ask 'How much can I get away with?' It is not only that most human systems will break down at some point, good people finding them burdensome while bad people find legal scope for their activities. One can try to put this right by perfecting the particular rules. It is rather that however wise and carefully adjusted for individuals a rule is, it is still in the last resort something external. It may leave practically no loopholes for the unscrupulous, but still keeping it is a different kind of thing from acting in a certain spirit. For example, if my enemy strikes me, the natural human thing for me to do is to hit back. If I hit back harder than he hit me that is unfair and wrong: this is the kind of thing that people rightly make rules about. Most societies recognize that private revenge leads to chaos and forbid people to do their own hitting back; but the corollary of this is a judiciary and police force to do it for them. To have a rule against hitting back, not for social reasons but for the good of the individual soul, is useless, for it does not stop the one thing that is really bad for one's soul, wanting to hit back.

Therefore, it is often said, make the rules internal: teach people that the true law is not concerned only with one's deeds but with one's inmost thoughts, and that this is what counts, not external obedience. This, we are told, is what Christ taught: his law was the law prophesied by Jeremiah which was to be written on the heart,[19] and that is the distinctive feature of his teaching. But unfortunately this interpretation takes us straight back into the difficulties which an objective system of law is supposed to avoid. Where a monastic community or a Church establishes an objective system it is claimed as an advantage that this is external to the individual; yet now we are recommended to go back to the internal law which led to spiritual pride or scrupulosity. Whatever it means to say that Christ's law is 'written on the heart' it cannot mean this.

---

[19] Jeremiah 31: 33.

CHAPTER 3

Law and Gospel

MANY sincere Christians believe that Rigorism is an entirely mistaken way of trying to interpret Christ's teaching. There is a strong school of thought which holds that his commands are not laws at all, but general principles and ideals which he laid before us to make us think, to show us the spirit in which we ought to act and the perfection at which we ought to aim. This point of view has been clearly and persuasively argued by the Provost of Sheffield and Canon Bryan Green.[1] They urge that 'Our Lord did not legislate or provide a new moral code of detailed precepts or rules which must be invariably followed. Rather He flung down uncompromising principles of right conduct, absolute and unqualified in their demands, and left it to his followers to work out the application in the relativities of their daily lives.'[2]

This approach is most illuminating, and goes a long way towards supplying the answer to the problem, but it has serious dangers. If we say that Christ did not provide 'detailed precepts' which must be 'invariably followed' we inevitably suggest that we may sometimes disobey his precepts. It would be different if he had merely laid down general principles, leaving us to apply them to reality; but his most characteristic teaching is concrete and explicit. For example, 'Whoever says, "You fool!" shall be liable to the hell of fire'[3]; 'Every one who looks at a woman lustfully has already committed adultery with her in his heart'[4]; 'Do not swear at all'[5]; 'If any one forces you to go one mile, go with him two miles'[6]; 'Do not be anxious about your life, what you shall eat or what you shall drink, nor about your body, what you shall put on.'[7] These are definite precepts, not generalities. They seem to make a clear and absolute demand. If we are to say that

---

[1] J. Howard Cruse and Bryan Green, *Marriage, Divorce and Repentance in the Church of England.*
[2] ibid., p. 27.
[3] Matthew 5: 22.
[4] ibid., 28.
[5] ibid., 34.
[6] ibid., 41.
[7] ibid., 6: 25.

they are not laws we must have some explanation to give of what they are and in what way they are to be obeyed.

The answer of course is that we are to live in the spirit of keeping these commands, but this does not take us very far. With commands as definite as this it is hard to see how living in the spirit of keeping them can mean anything different from actually keeping them. If they are not to be taken quite literally or obeyed always it becomes necessary in practice to specify when they need and when they need not be kept, and this means both weakening Christ's teaching and also not escaping from legalism after all.

I should like to maintain that the right interpretation is to be found by considering the crucial question of the nature of law in its relation to Christian morality. Now we have an explicit saying of Christ about what law is for : we have it, he told us, for our hardness of heart.[8] He was speaking of the law about divorce, but the principle can be applied much more widely and means, I believe, that laws are made for the just ordering of human affairs, since human beings cannot be trusted to live in peace spontaneously. For example, people are naturally revengeful when they have been injured, and the law of Moses, recognizing this, limited revenge to an eye for an eye and a tooth for a tooth.[9]

Unfortunately it is very easy for a Christian to see the law of Moses the wrong way round and so to misunderstand it. If one starts with the New Testament and looks on the Sermon on the Mount as one's Ten Commandments, the status of the old law of 'eye for eye, tooth for tooth' is bound to seem extremely puzzling. Clearly in some sense it has been superseded by Christian morality, but Christ did not deny that it was God-given; on the contrary, he came not to destroy but to fulfil it.[10] We can hardly suppose that God gave an inferior law to His people in, as it were, a moment of weakness, giving them permission to do things which were definitely wrong as a sort of reluctant concession to their 'hardness of heart,' a concession which at the first suitable moment He would withdraw.

If, on the other hand, we do not start with the Gospel but with human nature, and see it realistically as contaminated with a great deal of folly and wickedness, the law appears in its proper place as a

[8] Mark 10 : 5.
[9] Exodus 21 : 24.
[10] Matthew 5 : 17.

limitation and regulation of hardness of heart, not as a concession to it. The significance of an eye for an eye and a tooth for a tooth was not that people were allowed to exact harsh punishments from their enemies but that they were not allowed to exact unjust ones. This idea of a law which is 'just' makes very little sense as a kind of diluted version of Christian love, but it makes very good sense as an answer to the problem of human hard-heartedness. It is a fact, not a theory, that human beings seem to have some grasp of the idea that certain demands are reasonable and proper. Different peoples have wildly different ideas about *what* demands are just; but the idea of justice itself, as something which may fairly be required of one and which in turn one may fairly expect, seems to be natural to the human race.

The systems of law in which this concept of justice is embodied are extremely variegated. Some are thought of as divine, some as natural, some as man-made. Some are formal, some are informal. Some lawmakers aim at establishing rights for every one, others only at defending what they take to be rights of their own; but in the organization of human affairs it is nearly always right of some kind to which appeal is made.

In our society the most conspicuous lawmaker is the State, but it is by no means the only one. Apart from smaller bodies within the State, such as schools and clubs, making laws for their own members, there is public opinion, whose laws we feel to be quite as binding in their own way as the law of the land. Its sanctions are different, but the distinction it makes between the permissible and the forbidden is the same. Public opinion legislates about such things as not being mean, not being 'immoral,' keeping one's temper, and keeping one's place in a queue. Some of its laws are often more highly regarded than some of the laws of the land. For example, people are inclined to be more shocked by rudeness than by parking offences or petty smuggling.

It is usual to distinguish offences against the law of the land as 'crimes' whereas other offences are called 'sins,' and recently there has been a good deal of public discussion about where the boundary between these should be drawn.[11] People differ about whether certain kinds of actions, which they fully agree to be 'wrong,' are the business of the State and whether it is justifiable or desirable for the State to punish

[11] See e.g. The Wolfenden Report (Stationery Office, Cmnd. 247); Sir Patrick Devlin, 'The Enforcement of Morals,' Maccabean Lecture on Jurisprudence (British Academy), 1959; Professor H. L. A. Hart, 'Immorality and Treason,' *The Listener,* July 1959.

them. But for our present purpose the significant point is the similarity, not the distinction, between the different kinds of law which we find to be binding upon us. What they all have in common is that they set standards of decent behaviour which people feel they may reasonably require of one another, and lay down systems of rights and duties, the whole object of which is to be fair.

Now Christianity is not 'fair.' Christ's demands exceed legality, and ask more of us than can 'reasonably' be expected. Law requires, for example, that a man takes only what is his due, that he limits revenge to the claiming of suitable damages, that he only fights in self-defence and that he does not arbitrarily abandon his innocent wife. If more is asked of him than that he will have some justification for replying 'Why should I?' Yet the teaching of Christ is rather that a man does not insist even on his rights, that he loves his enemies, that he turns the other cheek, and that he remains faithful to his wife for better or worse. If we are meant to keep these requirements as laws our case is hopeless. If St. Paul could not attain to righteousness under the law of Moses,[12] how can we hope to do under a stricter law still? And if we are meant to enforce these requirements as laws on other people we shall inevitably find ourselves either being uncharitable or compromising our principles.

It is no help to say that Christ was only setting ideals before us rather than laying down inflexible laws. The ideals are meant to become actual : we are to be 'perfect.' The answer is that this can be achieved only by transcending law entirely. Christian morals are a Way, not a code : the Christian spirit does not consist in keeping the rules better than other people nor in keeping stricter rules, but in going beyond rules altogether. If people achieve the spirit of Christian love questions of their rights do not arise and it becomes possible and indeed natural for them to realize the New Testament ideals. They will act according to Christ's teaching; but not by a moral struggle to obey a difficult law.

To many people this idea sounds completely unrealistic; but it may seem less so if we remember that there is one situation in which ordinary human beings do often succeed in transcending rules, and that is happy family life. A mother does not ask, 'How little need I spend on presents for my children?' 'How much may I punish them for being naughty?' or 'What is it my duty to give my husband to eat?' She may find it difficult to decide how much it would be best to spend or punish or

12 Romans 7 : 22–4.

provide, but this is not a problem of law, and as soon as it becomes one of law she is to that extent not behaving like a mother or a wife. Her husband and children have legal rights against her which can be enforced, but nobody remembers this as long as family life is working normally; and in the really happy family even moral rights are forgotten and the members of the family live harmoniously, not from duty, but from a loving spirit. This is a quite familiar and not exceptional situation. Christianity therefore in asking us to transcend law is not talking about something of which we have no experience. It is taking a situation we have seen, happy family life, and using it as a model for our behaviour in general.

'Happy family life' may not sound much like the ascetic moralistic religion which is many people's idea of Christianity, but it is one of the most fundamental Christian ideas. It is the plain meaning of the Fatherhood of God and the brotherhood of man. The point is not that Christianity sets more store by human family life than it does by other values : to say this would be untrue. It is rather that distinctively Christian conduct depends, in the same way as family life depends, on personal relationships which have already been achieved. First people love each other, and then they find it natural to treat each other better than law requires. We can see in ordinary families that this order makes sense in practice; we can also see that to try to reverse it is useless. People do sometimes try to create love in their families by making loving conduct compulsory; what they actually create is artificiality at best and at worst estrangement.

This is not the situation in most families, for natural human affection is very strong. Loving personal relationships do exist and can be built on. The Christian Gospel, if I understand it rightly, is the good news that what is natural but partial in our families can become universal, that through God's act human beings have been reinstated as God's children and can achieve the spirit of love through which they can transcend law. To treat Christianity as if it were itself a new law to be obeyed instead of a new system of personal relationships to be entered into is, as it were, to sidetrack the Holy Spirit.

But to insist that Christian morals are personal morals and that the Christian Way transcends law does not mean that law itself is invalid, anomalous, or unchristian. We might rather call it sub-Christian. We are certainly not to think that Christianity justifies us in breaking the ordinary rules of moral behaviour. On the contrary, it should enable us to keep them better. Christ is 'the end of the law' [13] in the sense of liberating morality from legalism, but at the same time he did not come to destroy the law but to fulfil it.[14]

This way of understanding the relationship between law and Christian morality enables us to understand a number of apparently conflicting Christian ideas. From the point of view of the Gospel the Jewish law is apt to appear in contradictory lights as God-given, yet inadequate, yet a heavy burden. These are compatible if we look on it as a system of justice through which a people could learn its basic moral duty, a preparation for the spirit of love, not a substitute for it. If law is not a sort of first draft of Christian morality but fulfils a different function there is no paradox in saying that both can be God-given. It is when law is expected to exceed its function and take the place of love that it becomes a burden; and it is when it is looked on as complete in itself that it does not go far enough. This applies not only to the Jewish law but to any system, formal or informal, which lays down what is to be required of people, whether it is the 'law of nature,' [15] the code of honour of some particular group, or the law of a modern state. Any of these can be in accordance with God's will, or even be the result of divine guidance, without being therefore a direct way into the Kingdom of Heaven.

It follows that there is nothing particularly anomalous about the position of the Christian legislator, civil servant or judge. Like any other Christian layman he has a certain sort of work to do to which it is his duty to apply himself with integrity and goodwill. His Christianity will affect the whole spirit in which he works, but his work itself is still secular, not religious. A pious baker, one hopes, will bake more delicious and more wholesome cakes, and refuse to lend himself to any unfair tricks in making or selling them, but he will not therefore be baking pious cakes. If he comes to the conclusion that his cakes are somehow corrupting his customers he will stop selling them, but he will not foist something quite different upon them under the name of cakes. In the same way the pious statesman or lawyer will be more just and conscientious and try to make better laws because of his religion, but he will not therefore make pious laws. He need not see the administration of secular justice as a sort of half-hearted administra-

[13] Romans 10 : 4.
[14] Matthew 5 : 17.
[15] cf. Romans 2 : 14–15.

tion of divine justice, and he is not trying to come as near as he dares to the organization of a theocracy. He is trying to establish what is objectively fair. He is therefore not betraying Christian principles when he authorizes a punishment, condemns a criminal, allots damages, or grants a divorce. He is assigning to other people their legal and indeed moral rights. It is not for him to deny rights, to forgive other people's debts, or try to make Christian ideals compulsory. To attempt it is not merely practically difficult : it is a logical mistake. The step beyond justice requires something more than legality.

This does not mean that the 'something more' is only a kind of optional extra which some people can undertake in order to be specially good : on the contrary, the 'something more' is what the whole of Christian morals is really about. The present view therefore needs to be distinguished from the traditional theory of the 'double standard' which teaches that a certain necessary minimum of good behaviour is required of all Christians and that over and above the minimum it is possible to do 'works of supererogation' which are admirable but not compulsory.[16] The 'double standard' view divides moral exhortations into precepts and counsels, precepts which are binding upon everybody and counsels which are for those who have reached a more advanced stage and hope to acquire positive merit. The usual objection is that this involves the idea of a kind of spiritual aristocracy, in which the full heights of the Christian life are reserved for a chosen few; but Dr. Kirk in *The Vision of God* pointed out that this can be answered, provided that we look on the two standards as two successive stages. We may start, he said, by obeying the precepts but hope that the counsels in their turn will become 'precepts or immediate duties by-and-by.'[17] But the real objection is that even modified in this way the 'double standard' theory remains radically legalistic : when the 'counsels' do become 'precepts' we have in no way transcended law, morality is still a matter of keeping rules in the end after all, and those who take it seriously will be back in the vicious regress.[18]

The only way in which the highest morality can really be for everyone, or indeed for anyone, is by being a matter of personal relationships and not of rules. It is by trying to please another person out of love that one can really be set free from self-centredness, not by trying

[16] cf. The Thirty-Nine Articles of 1562, No. XIV.
[17] p. 243.
[18] See above, p. 22.

to 'be good.' A child who is happy and secure in his parents' love will simply want to please them and will co-operate in the way they are bringing him up without the question of priggishness ever arising. In the same way, if we can properly look on God as a loving Father rather than as primarily a law-giver this gives us a motive of action which is not self-regarding.

It may be objected that goodness is still to be achieved by obedience to a law, the supreme law of all, 'Thou shalt love the Lord thy God.' This law cannot be kept mechanically, and cannot lead to spiritual pride nor to scrupulosity. This is true and important, and raises questions to which we must return later [19]; but it is true because it is a very curious kind of law. What it commands is the spirit in which it is to be kept, so that it can only be kept at all by being transcended. It is not possible to set about loving God in the way in which one can set about keeping particular rules.

In fact this law needs to be 'written on our hearts' [20]; and now we are in a position to offer an interpretation of what this means. Christians have often understood the Gospel teaching as the fulfilment of Jeremiah's prophecy [21] : 'I will put my law within them, and I will write it upon their hearts; and I will be their God, and they shall be my people'; but if this is supposed to mean merely that we are to bring our inmost thoughts as well as our actions under the control of rules it is not 'good news' at all. It is the introduction of a harder moral standard before we have even learnt to maintain the older easier one. It only becomes 'good news' if we interpret it as the message that the keeping of God's law is to become natural to us, God Himself enabling us to do His will spontaneously because we are His own people. What we are promised is a personal relationship with God : 'And no longer,' the prophecy continues, 'shall each man teach his neighbour and each his brother, saying, "Know the Lord," for they shall all know me, from the least of them to the greatest, says the Lord.' Christians believe that this new relationship is made possible, in some way which we do not necessarily fully understand, by the life, death and resurrection of Jesus Christ. To believe the Gospel is to enter this relationship. Christian morality follows. It is not just a law which has to be kept; it is not just an ideal which we try to realize; it is the way people live when they are conscious of being the children of God.

[19] See below, p. 81.
[20] See above, p. 25.
[21] Jeremiah 31 : 33.

33

C

CHAPTER 4

A Personal God

TO say that Christian morality is a matter of personal relationships with God does not mean that all Christians ought to have 'religious experiences' of a special mystical kind. Plenty of good Christians would not claim to have any specific 'religious experiences' of this sort at all, and find mysticism a puzzling and even a disturbing phenomenon. It is surely possible to believe in God and try to serve Him without anything which could be called 'direct knowledge' of Him. No doubt people will have 'religious experiences' in Heaven, but not necessarily on earth. To suggest, as devotional writers sometimes do, that one cannot be a real Christian without in some small way beginning to be a mystic is far more likely to cause distress of mind or scepticism than to help people in their religion.

Yet to talk about a 'personal relationship with God' is by no means a piece of meaningless religious jargon committing one to practically nothing. It does not imply anything about mysticism, or about what kind of knowledge of God human beings must have, but it does imply a good deal about God. If we can rightly say that our relationship with Him is the essence of Christian morals He must be a Being with Whom personal relationships are possible and appropriate, that is, He must Himself be personal.

We already know that our fellow human beings are personal, that they feel and think and love and hate and have their own point of view. They are not waxworks or gramophone records or ideas in our minds, but people. If we cannot rightly say something like this about God then it cannot make sense to talk about entering into personal relationships with Him, for a genuine personal relationship essentially has two sides. Otherwise it is like a telephone conversation with nobody at the other end of the line. God may be much more than any person we can imagine, but if there is any real point in calling Him our Heavenly Father He must at least be like a person in being an independent Consciousness with His own divine point of view : He must be Someone rather than something.

Historically Christianity is undoubtedly founded on this basic belief

34

in a personal God. For the Jews God was the living God, in Whose image man is made. Christ himself, speaking to Jews, was able to assume this basis and go on from it to his own teaching, without having to begin by establishing the doctrine of a personal God. He certainly spoke very directly to God and about Him as a distinct personal Being, that is as our Father; so that if one believes that Christ was divinely inspired, still more if one takes him to be the Son of God, this way of speaking about God has the highest authority.

Yet none the less this doctrine of a personal God is far from being a religious commonplace. To affirm it, as Jews and Christians do, already represents a considerable theological commitment, and one which by no means everyone, nor even every religious man, is willing to undertake. There are religions, or at least religious attitudes to life, for which belief in a personal God is not essential. For example, classical Buddhism can be described as an 'atheist religion'; and there are many forms of pantheism where the whole universe, or Nature, is looked on with a sort of religious awe and reverence but is not held to be a separate conscious Being with a mind and will of His own. To many people, including some who would greatly like to call themselves Christians, the idea of a religion without a personal God has a certain apparent sophistication which makes 'the God of Abraham, Isaac and Jacob' seem anthropomorphic, naïve and childish in comparison.

These people are often warm admirers of the Christian way of life but at the same time deeply suspicious of dogma. They find the Christian doctrine of God utterly unconvincing and irrelevant, and yet they feel it important not to be left without any religion at all; so to adopt a non-personal idea of God in order to ward off atheism seems a very tolerable compromise. They therefore describe God as some kind of Force, Power or Idea rather than a Person. In particular they would like to prise Christian morals loose from Christian doctrine and be followers of Christ without insisting strictly on any Creed. The religion which results is not one which looks to a transcendent God to intervene and help us in our difficulties, or to another life in Heaven where wrongs will be made right. Instead it will lay stress on those passages in the Gospels which speak of being made one with God and with one another, and it will emphasize that the Kingdom of Heaven is within us.[1] In this way people hope that they can preserve the sense of wonder and reverence which a religious faith gives, they need not reject as

[1] e.g. Wisdom, 'Gods,' printed in *Logic and Language,* ed. Flew, p. 206.

delusions all ideas of holiness in which people have found inspiration, and above all they can still keep the Christian ideal of love and try to follow the Christian Way. If a man believes in 'Christian values' and the brotherhood of man, and maintains a respectful and sympathetic attitude towards religious practices they will consider him a true Christian and expect him to be as moral, more honest-minded, and much more easy to live with than the rigid theologian who takes every article in the Creed in its most literal sense.

This non-dogmatic religion may sound very adult and very reverent, but it is less coherent in itself, and abandons much more of Christianity than people often suppose. On the one hand the idea of a non-personal God is not really satisfactory. To speak of God as if He were simply another person like our friends and acquaintances certainly has an irreverent sound about it; but it is not easy to see what there is higher than a person to which we can liken Him more worthily. Unless we are to fall back upon a comparison with some inanimate being or collection of beings we can only suggest that He is like some abstract concept such as beauty or goodness. And of course He has often been so compared, and there is much value in the comparison; but taken on its own, without more personal ideas to correct it, it has a fatal weakness. An abstract concept cannot reciprocate personal relationships, any more than can a material object. Just as we may love a tree, but a tree cannot love us unless some personal spirit animates it, so we may love goodness but goodness cannot love us. Even love cannot love us, unless Love is personal; whereas a dog, a small child, a mature human being can enter into genuine two-sided personal relationships with us in increasing degrees, according to the extent to which they have personalities of their own. No doubt it is most inadequate to think of God as a very mature human being, but it does at least safeguard one of the main things which the Gospel teaches about Him, that He wishes us to enter into personal relationships with Him. Our idea of God is bound to be limited: what matters is that we should not limit it in any artificial way, or deny Him the highest reality we can think of because we are sure it is not high enough. If we are so afraid of belittling Him that we refuse to call Him personal we may well find ourselves thinking of Him as less than personal; and this is either idolatry or atheism.

Secondly, the Christian doctrine of God is a much more integral part of the Christian Gospel than people often suppose. Those who find it really incredible ought not to think that they have only cast off

an awkward and unnecessary superstructure. Christianity did not begin
as a message that we ought to behave in a certain way and reverence
certain ideals : it was first preached as the Good News that God had
personally intervened in history to reconcile men to Himself. It was by
accepting this that people could enter the Kingdom of Heaven. To
become a Christian was to become a child of God, not just to adopt
a certain moral policy.[2] People may think the good news false or un-
interesting, but it is only fair to admit that this is to reject the main
thing the early Christians thought they were talking about.

The anti-dogmatist may reply that even if he looks on the stories of
Christ's life, death and resurrection as fairy stories, at least there remains
a sublime system of morals. What matters to him is whether the Way
which Christ taught is a good way; and up to a point he is absolutely
right. The orthodox believer ought certainly to agree with the un-
orthodox here that if Christian principles are valid at all they must be
valid in their own right, with or without any supernatural backing. The
orthodox Christian is fortunate enough to be able to believe that they
have in fact been divinely vindicated; but for those who cannot accept
this there remains the respectable and indeed honourable position that
there is after all no good news but that Christian principles are still the
highest mankind has ever known and are to be followed to the bitter
end for their own sake.

This is noble : one may indeed call it quixotic if one remembers that
humanly speaking Jesus Christ was a first century man whose ideals
failed to such an extent that his followers all deserted him and he died
a failure. If some kind of Christianity without dogma is to have any
claim on the allegiance of twentieth-century people it is necessary for
it to put tremendous weight on the absolute excellence of Christian
ideals as such. This the anti-dogmatist is quite willing to do; and it is
here that he is confronted by a great difficulty. To try to follow Christianity, taking it as primarily a set of moral principles, still valid
although its Founder died long ago, is to return to legalism by losing
sight of the personal character of Christian ethics. 'Christian principles'
are only a step away from Christian laws and raise all the same questions about whether they are optional or compulsory, whether people
ought to be blamed for not following them and so on. The moralist
cannot permanently keep his mind shut to these questions without being

---

[2] cf. Braithwaite, 'An Empiricist's View of the Nature of Religious Belief,'
Eddington Memorial Lecture, 1955.

either naïve or obstinate; yet to give answers to them is destructive of the Christian spirit. A limited and regulated love of one's neighbour, however high we set the limit, is not a Christian love. Yet on the other hand to demand utter unselfishness as morally binding upon every one is to fly in the face of all reasonable moral judgment and go back to scrupulosity, pride and censoriousness. If it is a moral system we want we must have a fair one, and for this Christianity will not do. We cannot in all honesty say that as a matter of morals people can rightly be expected to suffer all manner of wrongs, and blamed if they will not. It is only if some kind of two-sided personal love and loyalty comes into the question that there develops a new kind of obligation which goes beyond justice; but this new obligation cannot be formulated into a system or detached from the relationship on which it depends.

It may well be asked at this point whether we cannot have a personal morality without God. We can certainly love each other without knowing God : indeed it is much more a question whether we could possibly know God at all without knowing human love already.[3] But natural human love often stops a long way short of the full Christian ideal. It is quite true that there are some people who seem to put the idea of the brotherhood of man into practice although their belief in the Fatherhood of God is shadowy in the extreme, and these are the people whom Christ commended rather than the cold-hearted religious believers : inasmuch as they minister to the unfortunate they are really ministering to him.[4] The trouble is that there are also vast numbers of people to whom the brotherhood of man is anything but real, who love their families and who are quite willing to do their duty to the rest of mankind but see no particular reason to do anything more. To these people on the human level there is no obvious appeal that can be made. To a man who is asking 'Why should I go out of my way to help this stranger?' it is no more persuasive to say 'He is your brother' than to say 'You ought to be good to every one.' It is different if he already believes in God as his Father. Then a total stranger can be seen as 'the brother for whom Christ died,'[5] and this is a fresh aspect of the situation to which appeal can be made.

It may still be objected that it is no more satisfactory to love other people for God's sake than to love them for a rule. People do not want

[3] 1 John 4: 20.
[4] Matthew 25: 34–46.
[5] 1 Corinthians 8: 11.

to be loved for somebody else's sake any more than they want to be loved on principle : what they really want is to be loved for themselves. It is quite true that if the would-be Christian who does things 'for God's sake' is really acting on a sort of concealed law or maxim his morality is after all no more personal than that of the honest atheist who feels obliged to leave God out of the question. But this need not be what the Christian is really doing. If by looking on other people as God's children he can come to see them as really lovable, he has found a way of genuinely enlarging the scope of his goodwill which someone who does not believe in a heavenly Father lacks. There is all the difference in the world between trying to love another person on principle and approaching him sympathetically because he is dear to someone one loves. The goodwill which results is real and unforced and therefore acceptable. It is uncontaminated by priggishness or condescension.

If on the other hand someone simply does not believe in God as his heavenly Father this particular link between himself and a stranger is lacking. He may happen to be a naturally warm-hearted benevolent person, but if he is not he cannot make himself so by forcing his feelings. Nor is it 'just as good' if he acts a compulsory benevolence he does not feel. If he is not kind by nature he can be just by rule, but neither of these is Christian charity. This is what it means, or at least this is what it should mean, to say that Christian morals are essentially based on the Christian doctrine of God : if God is not our heavenly Father in some significant sense, there is no particular reason why morality should transcend bare justice, except for those who feel so inclined.

It is important to make this clear, because it can easily be extremely misleading to say that Christian doctrine is the basis of Christian morals. It does not mean that morality collapses unless goodness will one day be vindicated by God and badness punished : this makes doing right merely a matter of self-interest. Nor does it mean that morality depends on the arbitrary will of God and is just the sort of thing He happens to like, which might have been different : this makes God a tyrant and goodness again a matter of self-interest, of keeping in favour at court. God has commanded His servants to be kind to one another; but on this view He might equally have commanded them to be cruel.

One must also beware of the idea that if Christian morality depends on doctrine then the atheist or agnostic must be wicked or at least amoral. Many sceptics are far more seriously and deeply concerned with morality than many practising Christians, and the integrity of a sceptic is particularly to be respected since he cannot expect any supernatural reward for it. An atheist can be as just, as honest, and as concerned with right and wrong as a Christian, but his difficulty comes when he tries to go beyond justice. Unless he happens to have a blinding devotion to some person or cause outside himself, in which case he runs the risk of one-sidedness, it is hard to see how he can avoid becoming pharisaical. For example, it is worth noticing how often in secular discussions of moral philosophy the argument turns to questions about when people are to be blamed or not to be blamed. A man who believes in God is in an easier position, but not for the reasons which are often assumed. It is not chiefly that he gains a moral standard which he would not otherwise have, nor that his morality is backed up by the promise of rewards and punishments, nor even that grace as a sort of moral stiffening gives him supernatural help in doing right. What he primarily gains is a living Person to follow Who is not one-sided but concerned with the whole world, in Whose service he has the chance to forget himself.

There is one other thing which we must beware of saying here. We must not say that because Christianity offers this, therefore Christianity must be true. The Good News might perhaps be too good to be true. The Person Whose love could do so much for us might not exist at all. To find out whether He does is a matter for Christian apologetics, not for Christian ethics, and our hope that He does ought to be recognized as a hope but not presumed on. We have no right to believe a doctrine simply because we like it, but only because we think it true; but if we do think it true, whether from personal experience, intellectual reasoning, trust in someone else, or a combination of these, it is right to emphasize that this truth is capable of transfiguring our morality.

CHAPTER 5

Law and the Family

IF God is our Father this means that the Kingdom of Heaven is more like a family than a state. Some theologians would lay great stress on the doctrine that we are not God's children by nature, but by adoption; but this makes the point even stronger. The whole object of adoption is to create a family which does not otherwise exist, so that personal relationships are the basis of an adopted family even more than of a natural family. The family exists for the sake of the relationships, and they make it a genuine family. It is artificial in origin, but becomes a legal and personal reality. To say someone is an adopted son is to say something actually true about him, not 'merely symbolic.' There is a great deal in the New Testament to suggest that we ought to think of our filial relationship to God in this way,[1] and it is quite compatible with the present theory.

On the other hand, there is also a great deal which seems to belittle the family. Some of Christ's hardest sayings are of this kind. He told his disciples that they would have to reject their families,[2] and predicted that family life would even suffer from his coming.[3] Nor did he always deal gently with his own relations.[4] Provided however that we may take all this as starting with a basis of intensely strong family feeling, it even helps to establish my point. Family affection is essentially natural but limited. It is easy to love the people we belong to in a fairly unselfish way,[5] and this kind of love is not specifically Christian but is a sort of ready-made model or pattern, in miniature, of what Christian love is like. To lead a Christian life is to put into practice the idea that the whole of mankind is God's family.[6] For a few this may even mean the repudiation of their own family ties; but for every one of these there are hundreds who need to remember that family affection is meant to be a starting point but not a stopping point.

Here we must face an obvious objection to this whole line of thought :

[1] e.g. Galatians 4: 5.
[2] e.g. Matthew 10: 37; Luke 14: 26. See above p. 11, note 2.
[3] e.g. Matthew 10: 34–6; Luke 12: 51–3.
[4] e.g. Mark 3: 33.
[5] Matthew 5: 46–7.
[6] See the Collect for Good Friday.

if the Christian Way is an extension not of justice but of our natural human affections then it is not a form of morality at all. Christianity seems to have nothing to do with obligation: duty becomes something non-Christian, and it even appears that we ought not to talk about 'Christian morality' any more than we talk about family love as 'family morality.' This problem of how the Christian Way is related to duty will recur when we come to consider what 'duty to God' means, but for the present we may accept the paradox, with reservations. It is partly a matter of what words we like to use. It would be very inconvenient not to be able to talk about Christian morals when we are discussing what qualities a Christian finds admirable, what states of affairs he thinks desirable, or what values would be realized in the Kingdom of Heaven. These are moral questions, and they are also Christian questions; but 'morality' in this sort of context does not mean something which can be put into a system, but simply a particular kind of topic or subject matter.

If on the other hand 'morality' is taken to be essentially something which can be reduced to a system of rules of right and wrong there is much to be said for the doctrine that the Gospel comes not to make us more moral but to liberate us from morality. Morality in this sense is what we need when love is limited. The problems which arise in a context of undoubted love are not generally seen as moral problems at all: 'What will be best for his future?' 'How can I be most help?' 'What would she prefer?' rather than 'What is my duty?' We may not even recognize this attitude as an example of 'the spirit of love' because it is so unselfconscious and remote from any kind of heroism. It certainly does not seem to deserve praise, although it may easily go well beyond the requirements of simple justice. It is this kind of love which Christianity endeavours to spread beyond its natural rather narrow limits. If it could be extended to include the whole of mankind, without spoiling its spontaneity and normality, the Kingdom of Heaven would be at hand. It may sound paradoxical to describe Heaven as a place where people never think about doing their duty; but we can see what it means if we try to imagine a Heaven where duty was a major concern. If we were constantly having to consider what we ought to do and continually engaged in moral struggles we should not be in Heaven at all.

The Christian Way, then, is not strictly speaking a form of morality; but this idea is easy to misunderstand and needs a little more explanation. It certainly does not mean that Christianity rejects all human morality as really evil. The idea that human justice is really injustice, and that human goodness is not merely imperfect but utterly corrupt, is both practically and theoretically objectionable. It is extremely un-plausible to say that human beings are as bad as this; and if they were they could never know it. If what we mean by good is really evil it is nonsense for us to talk about goodness at all or suppose that we have any right to say even that God is good. Christianity on the contrary presupposes that we are partly good, that we can recognize justice and that we have some loving impulses. If this were not so it would be useless to preach the Gospel, for we could never even understand, still less accept it.

The opposite misunderstanding is to suppose that Christianity does away with morality altogether, that Christians may do as they please and be utterly lawless. This is 'antinomianism.' It is a sort of caricature of genuine Christian doctrine; but it is a caricature which is so fre-quently brought into the argument that it is rather important to show what is wrong with it and what is the true position of moral rules for Christianity. Briefly, we may say that love cannot be reduced to law but that it still has law as a basis. Even if we imagine a community of people who are already perfect, to whom universal goodwill comes as naturally as partial goodwill does to us, the idea of right and duty does not become invalid.[7] It does become a rather difficult academic idea. To these people duty is part of what they want to do rather than something which constantly interferes with their desires, so it may be hard to single out; but a moral philosopher among them could still distinguish it. Law is swallowed up but not destroyed.

For people who are not yet perfect in this way it is all the more true that laws have a proper place. To see what this proper place is in Chris-tianity the family analogy is very helpful. The natural family has rules outside it and rules inside it, but it does not live by rules : the same is true of the Christian family.

Taking external rules first, it should be quite clear that members of the Christian family are just as much subject to the moral law as mem-bers of the Smith family are subject to the law of the land. In the family circle the law of the land will not normally impinge, but it is not

[7] Mr. Neil Cooper imagines such a community, which he calls a 'Community of Holy Wills,' in an article on 'Rules and Morality' in the Proceedings of the Aristotelian Society, Supplementary Volume XXXIII (1959), 'The Holy-Will-in-the-street just will not know what the word "ought" means,' he says (p. 167).

therefore repudiated. It remains binding and the members of the family know it is binding, if they ever stop to think about it. If after all one of them does repudiate it, it is all ready to step in. If family life collapses and John Smith murders George Smith he is at least as liable to the penalties of the law as if he had been a stranger. In the same way if a Christian tells lies to a fellow Christian he has simply put himself back under the moral law, as much as if he had never been a Christian : the spirit of love has been destroyed, but morality is as valid as ever.

Not only is the ordinary human family law-abiding in its relation to the outer world; it has an important place for rules of its own as well. To say that the Kingdom of Heaven is more like a family than a state does not mean therefore that the Kingdom of Heaven is a sort of anarchy. There are three chief purposes which rules serve in family life, and these apply whether we are talking about the natural family or the Christian family.

In the first place, rules and even the enforcement of rules are necessary in bringing up children. This is not a partial breakdown of the present theory, but on the contrary is a good illustration of the way law and love are related. Children seem to begin with a basic capacity for love, an equally basic selfishness, and a strong sense of justice. If out of these a loving spirit is to have a chance to develop it is essential not to suppose that justice and love are much the same thing, and equally essential not to dispense with justice prematurely. This is not only because selfishness will take over, although it certainly will, for an undeveloped capacity for love cannot be expected to resist selfishness without some external help. It is also because a state of affairs in which justice is not emphasized or is even belittled is positively unhelpful to a child. A parent who takes away a special toy and gives it to one of the other children in the name of brotherly love does not set an example of love, only of injustice; and a parent who leaves it to the children to fight it out in the hope that affection will prevail has simply neglected his own moral duty to teach them the basic principles of right and wrong. Love needs to be fostered, not presumed upon; and meantime the rule of some kind of acceptable law is immensely important not only to make life bearable but also to establish firmly the fundamental idea of justice. In this way a basis is created on which the love which transcends justice can properly be built. This is what happens in the ordinary human family, and the equivalent of it in the Christian family is that Law came before Gospel, the Old Covenant before the New. The children of Israel had to learn to be just before they could be expected to learn to be loving. So indeed would any individual who came to Christianity from a relatively amoral background.

This does not mean that before the spirit of love can be achieved there must first be a kind of tyranny in which rules are kept for fear of parents or God and severity takes the place of affection. Ancient Israel was not like this, and nor is the typical family. There is rather a far more complicated situation in which inextricably involved in the rule of law there are all kinds of foreshadowings of the rule of love which is to follow. On the one hand the parents do not have to wait for the children's love to develop before they can express their own love for their children. Indeed if they did wait the children's love would be stunted. Long before the coming of the Gospel the Jews under the Law were able to speak about the 'steadfast love' as well as the righteousness of God,[8] Who indeed had delivered them from Egypt before He legislated. The equivalent of God's loving-kindness in the human family is the spontaneous love parents have for their children, irrespective of whether the children behave well or badly. No doubt all human love is most imperfect and is often selfish or unwise, but at its best parental love in its complete devotion is, as we are told, the most authentic analogy for the love of God.[9] On the other hand, the children on their side show a capacity to respond to this kind of love. They begin to express a loving spirit spontaneously in all sorts of ways; and if this did not happen naturally they could never get beyond justice at all, however much they were loved. We cannot instil the loving spirit into people, we can only encourage it to grow.

Even when it has grown there remains a second reason why rules are needed in family life : they are necessary for practical convenience. The normal family is not legalistic, but neither is it chaotic. For example, people have to have some idea, however flexible, about when meals are to be available, and somebody has to be responsible for providing them. In the same way problems about who is to have some privilege or do some tedious job are much better solved by making a rule, such as to divide things out or take turns, than by arbitrary self-sacrifice however willing. Fairness does not rule out generosity; on the contrary, effective generosity is impossible if one does not know what is fair. All these

[8] e.g. Psalm 36: 7.
[9] e.g. Psalm 103, 13.

things are organized by laws, explicit or understood, but any one who thought the laws were there to make the family more loving, or that they were there to stop them falling to blows, would completely misunderstand what really holds the family together. Nor can we expect to recognize a happy family by how formal or informal it is. Sometimes family life is very orderly; sometimes much more emphasis is placed on spontaneity. There are people who like to have their meals at set hours in tidy clothes, and others who feel stifled if they cannot be casual. Both may be loving or unloving, but they express it in different ways. Similarly, we cannot expect to recognize a member of the Kingdom of Heaven by the extent to which he lives by rules. For somebody to love rules is a matter of temperament; it proves nothing either way about whether he loves other people.

Whether rules are looked on with enthusiasm or not, there is a third way in which they can be rather useful in family life : as a rough-and-ready guide to conduct. To insist on deciding every trivial case on its merits would be as much a form of scrupulosity as to have an absolutely rigid unbreakable rule. It is not only harmless but useful to have a number of general rules which in the ordinary way people simply keep without having to stop and think : 'Do not interfere with other people'; 'Do not hurt anybody'; 'Do not tell lies.' Most families will have a number of more specific rules too : 'Do not disturb Johnny when he is doing his homework'; 'Do not leave the landing light on all night.' The same is true of the Christian family : for instance, 'Do not talk loudly in church.'

The important thing is to be clear that these rules are useful, not sacrosanct. None of them is either absolute or sufficient. Possible exceptions may be invented for all of them; and even when they are all conscientiously kept love may still be entirely lacking. Above all, rules of this kind cannot be used as a way of deciding what to do in difficult cases, for if a difficult case has arisen the plain rule has already broken down. If the new case is different enough for the problem to be raised it may be different enough to need a new rule. It is merely begging the question to give oneself orders like 'Never tell lies' when the problem with which one is confronted simply is whether a lie should be told this time. But then, it may be said, in the plain case we do not need the rule : it might therefore appear that all moral rules of this sort are useless.

In fact they can be extremely useful, not as a way of making decisions but as a way of reminding oneself under stress of what one has already decided. They are a shield against temptation, not perplexity. 'Rules,' it has been said,[10] 'act as a warning against making exceptions in favour of oneself.' If for example one is tempted to tell a lie to get oneself out of trouble it is a help to have it firmly fixed in one's mind already that lying is wrong, so that one's natural instincts work against it. There is therefore no need to reject entirely the kind of system of rules described above,[11] in which the members of the Christian family have their lives regulated for them by their Church, so that they simply form a habit of living in an orderly and decorous fashion which gives them something to rely on in times of stress. We can allow for the use of this method of approach without at the same time letting in its abuse, for we can see it as essentially subordinate to the family spirit. It can be a great help to some kinds of people, but it is entirely a means to an end, not an end in itself. It should also be emphasized that it is a means to a rather limited end, leading a good life when it is quite clear what one ought to do, not finding out what one ought to do when real moral problems have arisen.

We can now see that the part which law plays in happy family life is by no means negligible, but it is much more like the oil in the engine than the petrol. It helps things to run smoothly and is sometimes essential to prevent a complete breakdown, but it ought not to be expected to supply the motive power.

What we have cast doubt on, therefore, is not the usefulness of rules but the usefulness of the science of casuistry. Casuistry on the whole is mistrusted for the wrong reasons. It is thought to be a rather dishonest way of finding excuses for not doing one's duty, whereas at its best it is a sincere attempt to illuminate moral problems by thinking clearly about them. The trouble is that the illumination is generally much more theoretical than practical. It is absorbingly interesting to try to see what it is about lying that makes it absolutely wrong and yet apparently justified in certain cases; but it is interesting because we already have in mind some examples of lies which we think are not wrong and want to find out what they have in common and what general principle will cover them all. It is a very different matter to try to apply our principles once formulated to a completely new problem where we do not already know what to think. What makes it a new problem is the very

[10] Macbeath, *Experiments in Living*, p. 381.
[11] p. 23.

fact that our existing rules do not apply properly to it. To try to force them to fit is to run a grave risk of getting the wrong answer, and theoretically the casuist recognizes this. He certainly does not want to apply his existing moral rules uncritically and rigidly to the new problems : on the contrary, he prides himself on not being a Rigorist, on understanding how circumstances alter cases and making every allowance for this.[12] But if one has to consider the circumstances, this means in the last resort the circumstances of the individual case. The significant features of a moral problem are the features which make it unique; and therefore although one can often decide in advance what to do one cannot decide in general. It may be said that this is most unsatisfactory; but then it may be asked in return why we should expect to be given a straightforward recipe for solving the fundamental problems of life. Difficult moral decisions are supposed to engage the whole personality; the responsibility cannot as it were be handed over from the conscience to the intellect.

[12] See e.g. Kirk, *Conscience and its Problems.*

CHAPTER 6

Morals beyond Law

THE conclusion that casuistry is not of great practical usefulness will not be readily accepted. People desperately want guidance, and to refuse to give them any rules and tell them that all they need to do is to act in the spirit of love can be positively offensive. But if we interpret 'the spirit of love' as 'the Christian family spirit' it is by no means an empty idea, and can give practical help in real problems where systems of rules break down.

For example, rules cannot be much help in deciding when it is right to tell a lie. To attempt to apply the rules come what may is really to treat external conformity as more important than basic honesty of purpose. If instead of worrying about rules we admit quite frankly to ourselves that what we want to do is to deceive someone, but remind ourselves that the person we want to deceive is in sober fact the child of God, we may begin to have some idea of whether God would want the lie told. On the one hand He would not want us to tell it lightly; but on the other hand He certainly would not want us to tell the truth just for the selfish reason of keeping our own souls pure when there were serious reasons in favour of lying. What ought to be considered is not only our own integrity but the integrity of the other person. We must therefore be suspicious both of a rigid refusal on principle to tell any lie and of an unscrupulous readiness to tell lies for people's 'own good' or because we think the consequences will be beneficial. For example, a friend asks in all seriousness 'Do you like this piece of work I have done?' or 'Am I dangerously ill?' and if we give him a favourable reply whatever the facts are we are somehow failing to honour him. If the favourable answer is also the true one we should not like to have to think, 'But I should have said that anyway.' Yet sometimes we may judge that the lie must be told : if we approach the question from the point of view of how God would wish His children to deal with one another we should be able to achieve a greater insight into its complexities. We may call this a new sort of casuistry if we must; but its aim is not to pick out the likeness between cases and so apply rules to

49

them, but on the contrary to see the uniqueness of each case and solve it as such.

The idea of the Christian family gives one not a set of rules to apply to situations but a practical ideal to live by. It is not easy, any more than happiness in natural families is easy, but it is realistic. Its great importance is that it brings the teaching of Christ within one's reach. This may sound presumptuous, since only the grace of God can really do that; but from the human point of view what people need to know is how they can best try to co-operate with God's grace.

For Christianity to be put into practice is sometimes a matter of ordinary people becoming capable of conspicuous heroism, but it is not always simply this. In a way heroism is more within one's reach than everyday goodness, for anyone can make an attempt at it if the necessity arises, by clenching his teeth and setting himself to perform the heroic act. It may be beyond him, but at least he knows how to try. The difficulty about some of Christ's commands considered as rules to be obeyed is that we do not even know how to try. Moral theologians assure us that Christian love is a matter of the will rather than the emotions, but in practice it is not much use to set out to love one's neighbour as oneself by a conscious moral effort. What is some use is to think of one's neighbour and oneself as both alike being children, perhaps not very satisfactory children, in God's family. Then one does not have to try to persuade oneself that one's neighbour is behaving well if he is not, but only to remember that God loves him too, that one is not always entirely lovable oneself, and that God will be all the more grieved if one makes bad worse by indulging in bitter feelings. In this way one has much more hope of arriving at a charitable understanding of other people.

We can now interpret Christ's sayings as positive illustrations of the way the Christian family spirit will show itself, rather than as set rules on the one hand or general principles on the other. He has given us literally examples, that is instances, of the way he wants us to behave. To say that he has given us an Example and that the Christian life is the imitation of Christ is therefore a partial truth, just as it is a partial truth to say that the Christian life is obedience. It is a more complete truth to say that to follow him is to treat him as Head of the family. Sometimes it is appropriate for us to imitate him directly: for instance, we can try to show patience in personal distress. Sometimes we are in a position simply to obey instructions : for instance, we can use the Lord's Prayer. Generally, however, accepting the authority of Christ is a matter of trying to please him in a much more complex and less straightforward way.

This interpretation of Christ's teaching is, I believe, the only method of avoiding the difficulties of Rigorism and yet still doing justice to the stringency of his commands. We cannot make them into laws, but he did mean them to be taken seriously.[1] A fundamental problem of Christian ethics arises here, the question of pacifism. We are accustomed to approach it legalistically, assuming that violence is forbidden but tempting and asking what limits we may concede to the duty of turning the other cheek. Sometimes we arrive at strict and sometimes at lenient answers, but we seldom really satisfy ourselves and still less each other, for there are always too many contrary arguments to explain away. It is more promising to ask, not what Christ would allow but what his wishes would be, for at once we have a better chance of seeing a situation as a whole and not just from the point of view of our individual righteousness. On the one hand we shall have to stop making excuses for simply disregarding his wishes in many everyday matters. It would be revolutionary if Christians were to stop acting on the assumption that provocation is a good reason for hitting back, stop bringing up their children to 'give as good as they get,' and abandon the idea that one must always defend one's rights; but it would certainly be a way of putting the Sermon on the Mount into practice. It can hardly be doubted that the true Christian spirit is profoundly pacifist in the sense of having a deep repugnance towards hatred and violence. On the other hand, we cannot make mechanical rules about how this repugnance is to be expected to show itself. If a man dies because I am too pure to use violence against his attacker I am responsible for an innocent death instead of a guilty one. This over-simple example shows how we take responsibility for events as much by our inaction as by our actions. A Christian ought always to ponder whether a particular gesture such as renouncing the use of violence is, in its context, the right way to witness to Christian ideals, or whether on the contrary it is a way of washing his own hands in innocence while actually inviting the violence he is seeking to witness against. In deciding what God wants us to do we cannot escape from the need to consider facts as well as principles.

To try to live as a member of the Christian family in this kind of way is a no less exacting but more possible and satisfactory enterprise

[1] See above, p. 26.

than to follow an intensely strict rule of life. If we take the idea of the family of God seriously we are in a far better position than the legalist to form a constructive picture of what a Christian really ought to be like. A prevalent idea of the good Christian is of a careful law-abiding man, meticulous in his religious observances, consciously pure and upright in all his dealings, and easily shocked. It is impossible to live in an ordinary human family for long without acquiring a rather different picture of which qualities are desirable and which destructive. If we think of human relationships as we experience them, without any pious prejudice, it is obvious for example that few people can make themselves more intolerable without meaning any harm than the person who fusses and the person who always has to be right. These are real sins into which people fall every day, yet there is a tendency for preachers and moralists to emphasize them less than many more theoretical ones. The significant fact is that the point of view one derives from normal family life is also thoroughly Biblical : 'Do not be anxious about to-morrow; to-morrow will look after itself. Each day has troubles enough of its own.' [2] 'There will be greater joy in heaven over one sinner who repents than over ninety-nine righteous people who do not need to repent.' [3] The person who is calm [4] but enthusiastic,[5] self-effacing [6] but available,[7] good company [8] but sensible,[9] humble [10] but effective [11] is exactly the sort of person we find lovable in family life and is also the sort of person that Christ's own teaching puts before us as admirable.

Not only do some neglected Christian virtues such as calmness and gaiety come into prominence if we look on Christian life as family life; but also some more traditional virtues such as asceticism and self-denial become easier to understand rightly. Christ clearly expected Christians to practice abstinence sometimes : 'The time will come when the bride-groom will be taken away from them, and on that day they will fast.' [12] Christian self-denial is not only a matter of training ourselves like athletes or soldiers, but also a matter of taking serious things seriously

[2] Matthew 6 : 34 (New English Bible); see also e.g. Luke 10 : 41–2.
[3] Luke 15 : 7 (New English Bible); see also e.g. 15 : 25–32.
[4] e.g. Mark 4 : 38–40.
[5] e.g. Matthew 13 : 44–6.
[6] e.g. Matthew 6 : 3.
[7] e.g. Mark 14 : 37.
[8] e.g. Matthew 11 : 19.
[9] e.g. Matthew 25 : 8.
[10] e.g. Luke 18 : 9–14.
[11] e.g. Luke 16 : 8; 19 : 12–26.
[12] Mark 2 : 20 (New English Bible); see also Matthew 6 : 16–18.

and showing reverence and respect. A good son will not go to a gay party on the day of his father's funeral, not because it is forbidden but because he will not want to. On the other hand he will not insist on his children dressing up in black and stop them from playing games when they are too little to understand : he will know that his father would not have wanted them to be unhappy. In the same way, if a young man's parents have made sacrifices to pay off their son's debts they will not want him to waste it all over again in riotous living, but nor will they want him to ruin himself to pay them back when the whole object of their sacrifice was to save him from ruin. If the sacrifice that has been made was the Sacrifice of the Cross a reverent Christian will for instance certainly not want to be frivolous on Good Friday; but if he tries to punish himself all the year round he is in effect repudiating what has been done for him.

It is much easier too for Christians not to judge one another and not to take pride in their own Christianity if they look on the service of God as a matter of filial love rather than primarily obedience to law. On the one hand one does not take pride in love; in fact the more one loves the less one is likely to take any credit for it. On the other hand one does not intrude into other people's love or expect to be able to judge the way they express it. To decide whether somebody is a good Christian is not like deciding whether he is a good citizen, which anybody may have a valid opinion about; it is like presuming to decide whether he is a good son or husband. It is not possible for people outside a particular relationship to know whether it is profound or superficial, or whether it is more or less satisfactory than it appears to the outside world. Some families are demonstrative, some inarticulate : one ought to respect other people's privacy and modesty in religion as much as in human relationships, and not expect all those who love God to be extroverts. Between the exhibitionism of those who love to pray at street corners and the cowardice of those who are afraid to practice their religion for fear of ridicule there are whole ranges of expression or reticence which are perfectly proper to a devout Christian. We can even see that it is possible for a man to be faithful without being obviously devout at all; whereas if conformity with religious law is the criterion we are bound to be troubled when we notice that plenty of apparently good people certainly do not conform. Just laws apply equally to every one, so that it is almost impossible not to have opinions about how they are being kept; but personal relationships are each unique, so that if we think of religion in this way we can give life to the platitude that other people's behaviour is not for us to judge.

All this does not mean that people can count themselves as faithful Christians whatever they do, any more than they can count themselves as good sons or good husbands whatever they do. The man who says 'My wife doesn't expect me to keep bringing her flowers' may be perceptively understanding that she hates outward show, but on the other hand he may be lazily presuming on her love. It is a question between himself and his wife, but a real question none the less.

Nor does it mean that a person's religion can be a completely solitary affair, any more than family love can be entirely a matter of separated exclusive relationships. Family life is something in which a number of people can join : brothers and sisters normally love their parents and each other together as well as separately. The most satisfactory personal relationships need not be cherished in isolation. Just as a happy marriage is not a withdrawal from the world but a kind of secure centre for other affectionate relationships, so a religious man's relationship with God is unique but not exclusive in the sense of shutting out the outer world. A love which has no privacy is shallow; but a love which excludes other people is possessive. 'Even the anchorite,' T. S. Eliot points out in *The Rock*, 'prays for the Church'; and the real Christian saint is the person who loves other people more profoundly and effectively because of his love for God.

In ordinary human affection people can often act as messengers of goodwill for one another, without any intrusion : 'She sent you her love'; 'I think he would be immensely touched if you were to write'; 'They were saying such nice things about you'; 'She was not at all offended.' Even an unpalatable message may on occasion be justified and helpful : 'I am afraid that made him very unhappy.' In the same way there is a place for messengers of goodwill in the Christian family, and this is surely a useful way for Christian evangelists to look on their task, whether they are preachers, parents teaching their children, or people trying to explain Christianity to their friends. They are not supposed to try to persuade other people to conform to a pattern, but rather to try to promote personal understanding. It is not irreverent to think of God as a real Person Who can be glad or sorry at what people do; indeed it is hard to see how else one could represent Him convincingly to somebody else.

Not only earthly Christianity but even the idea of Heaven itself becomes more comprehensible if we think of religion in terms of the best we know of human love rather than of the loftiest duty. Many people feel baffled by the concept of a completely non-competitive society, where one person's gain is not another person's loss, where one would be exactly as happy at the good fortune of somebody else as of oneself, where questions of selfishness would simply not arise. It becomes much easier if we remember that in happy human families the ideal is already partly realized. A whole family rejoices in the good fortune of one member; a husband and wife are utterly at a loss to decide which of them shall have some particular treat; a mother would far rather her children were given a delightful present than have one herself. It is not a question of giving up something to someone else, but of being identified with somebody else's happiness. In the Kingdom of Heaven this kind of identification with the happiness of other people would be unlimited.

There is a more serious difficulty about the next life which confronts any thinking Christian: the problem of whether the Christian doctrine of rewards and punishments, of Heaven and Hell, is morally satisfactory at all. It is a serious question whether in these basic and Biblical doctrines Christianity actually falls short of the best moral ideas of human beings. Eternal reward appears crude and eternal torment positively wicked; in many ways we can understand Purgatory best, only to find that it has much the least Biblical warrant. On consideration we may decide that any developed theory of Purgatory, of paying for our own sins, makes nonsense of the Atonement; but then we are left with the more terrible but undoubtedly Biblical doctrine of Hell, and with a horrifyingly narrow line between those who are allotted eternal happiness and those who are consigned to eternal misery.

These criticisms are basically twofold: that the penalties proposed for sin are excessive and therefore unjust; and that even if they could be seen to be just it is curious that God should ever enforce them instead of showing mercy, that He should be less forgiving than He expects us to be. It is hopeless to try to answer them by making debating points within a legalistic theory of the next world. To do this is to trifle with people's profound moral convictions.

It is much more promising to ask instead whether what happens in family life can make the Christian doctrine of Heaven and Hell more ethically comprehensible. It is clear that happy family life, with which

55

we are comparing Heaven, is not a system of rewards but of personal relationships; but none the less the personal relationships may be called the 'reward' of the way the members of the family live. People often describe family life as 'rewarding,' and Heaven is surely 'rewarding' in just this sense, not something extra meted out for being good but the profoundly satisfactory result of a certain way of life.

Conversely, unhappy family life is not a system of punishments but a severance of relationships. The breakdown of family love does not express itself in imprisonments and penalties but in divorces and estrangements. I suggest that this is what Hell means: not being harshly condemned to an eternal life sentence which might have been remitted, but rather cutting oneself off from family life. If family life in the last resort is the only life there is, to cut oneself off from it is destruction; and it is significant that the New Testament images for Hell, such as burning and decay,[13] are images of destruction much more obviously than of punishment. Retributive ideas are undoubtedly present,[14] but the primary emphasis is on a disastrous estrangement and separation.[15] This final severance of relationships, I believe, is the possible rejection of which Christ warned us. We may hope that it will not eventually happen to anybody, but we have been expressly told that it is a possibility, even for people who think themselves established in the centre of the family, if they lack the family spirit of love.[16] The seriousness of Hell remains; but the ethical doubt about it is much diminished if we look on it as the possibility of becoming incapable of family life rather than as the risk of being placed on the wrong side of a legal dividing line.[17]

[13] e.g. Mark 9: 48; Matthew 13: 30.

[14] e.g. Matthew 25: 46; Revelations 14: 9–11.

[15] To substantiate this all the difficult passages would need to be examined. For example the parable of Dives and Lazarus (Luke 16: 19–31) stresses the urgency of choosing while we can, and this urgency is not to be minimized; but the use of the conventional phrase 'Abraham's bosom' suggests, I think, that the Lord was making his point by means of a story, not talking literally about his Heavenly Father on giving us information about what the next life is like. In a similar way, though of course on a very different level, people tell stories beginning 'A man died and went to heaven, and St. Peter (not God) said to him . . .' It is clearly understood that these stories do not map out anybody's future life; if they are true to life their truth is of another kind.

[16] e.g. Matthew 7: 21–3.

[17] The Bishop of Woolwich has argued profoundly and convincingly that ultimately God's love will win every soul and Christ will indeed by all in all. (J. A. T. Robinson, *In the End, God.*) I am far from wishing to dispute this. But he also insists on the seriousness of damnation, since each of us has to make for himself the real and free choice between Heaven and Hell; and the point I should like to make is that damnation need not be a legal concept.

This theory of Heaven and Hell does not necessarily involve the conclusion that within the family the idea of punishment has no meaning. We have seen that the children of a family are still partly under law [18]; and in human families this nearly always means that they are sometimes punished. Most parents and educationalists agree that in bringing up children reformative punishment has a proper place, though they differ about how much and of what kind. We cannot guess and have not been told whether God approves of this for His family and whether a reformative Purgatory will form part of our spiritual upbringing.

Even if it does not, it does not follow that we shall all slip into Heaven in a facile way provided we have good intentions. Whatever the Biblical concept of Judgment means, it must mean that we shall know just what we have done, and what it has cost. If this means realizing that one has hurt somebody one loves it is in a way its own punishment, though not an externally imposed penalty. To face this kind of truth is the way to restore damaged personal relationships, but it is not a way of being let off cheaply. The Prodigal Son was not received back into his family on conditions, nor could he come back merely by 'meaning well.' For nearly every one arrival in Heaven must be the return of a prodigal : the cause of celebrations, but the result of facing the truth, repentance and forgiveness.

[18] p. 44.

CHAPTER 7

Law and the Church

IF the Kingdom of Heaven is a family, it does not immediately follow that we can say the same about the Church. The relationship between the Church and the Kingdom is a standard theological problem, but it is at least evident that they cannot be treated as simply identical, for in the Church as we see it the Kingdom of Heaven is certainly not fully realized. We cannot therefore automatically apply to the Church whatever we have said about the Kingdom: the question still needs to be discussed.

There is no need to deny that the Church can be a family simply because of its great size. Just as in human families there is a continuity of affection between one generation and the next although few people can remember all their great-grandparents, so in the Church there is continuity in space as well as in time, and it is possible for Christians who are never likely to meet to be related to each other as members of one body and share in the same family spirit. Church divisions break the outward continuity and spoil the spirit, but if the Church were united its size alone would not prevent it from being a family.

It is clear that the Church neither is nor aims at being entirely free from laws and rules; but then, as we have seen, neither is the family. It is possible as a preliminary to exhibit quite a close correspondence between the proper place of rules in the Church and their proper place in the family, and arrive at the provisional conclusion that the Church is like the family since it has laws outside it and laws inside it but does not live by laws.

In the first place, the Church has law outside it. If the members of the Church step outside the spirit of Christian love and begin to rob, cheat or murder each other they will have to be checked by law. These are not contingencies within family life, but only arise if family life breaks down.

Secondly, there is an important place for rules within the Church just as there is for rules within the family. They are needed for the immature, providing a basis of justice upon which the spirit of love can grow; for practical convenience; and for rough and ready guidance. For example, the Ten Commandments are part of the moral basis of Christianity; regulations about how services are to be conducted or what happens when a new incumbent has to be appointed are administrative arrangements; recommendations about how often to go to Church give practical guidance for the members of the Christian family. The life of the family, which is what really matters, is something which transcends all these. Unfortunately it is as easy for the Church as for human parents to over-emphasize law, to treat grown-ups or adolescents as children, to become devoted to rules which were once simply meant to be useful, to confuse means with ends.

A much greater difficulty is that the Church has frequently not been regarded in this way at all. The medieval Church has indeed been described quite frankly as a state [1]; and even in the modern world, when the Church is supposed to have abandoned temporal power and devoted itself to things spiritual, a great deal more legalism seems to be considered tolerable in it than is found in the average family. It seems presumptuous to characterize all this as simply an aberration. One can hardly argue: on the present theory the Church is a family, in fact it is much more legalistic than a family ought to be, therefore it must be overreaching itself. The answer might too easily be, so much the worse for the present theory. Nor can I undertake to discuss the whole course of Church history up to the present time to see how far the development of the legal attitude has prevented the Church from being a family, and how far this has meant that it has lost its true nature. It is too arbitrary to try to assimilate Church and family in this over-simple way. Instead I should like to suggest that the same kind of consideration which makes legalism inappropriate in the family applies also to the Church, and in this way to give reasons for looking on legalism in the Church with the utmost caution.

The basic contrast between the legal and the family spirit is not that a legal system has to be more rigid; plenty of happy families have set habits and strict rules. Nor is it even that laws are enforced by penalties: some families have quite severe punishments. The important difference is that law is concerned with duty and obligation rather than with personal relationships. If we like we can make our laws flexible to the point of inefficiency and the sanctions enforcing them mild to the point of being merely nominal, but the result of all this is a feeble set

---

[1] F. W. Maitland, *Roman Canon Law in the Church of England,* p. 100.

of laws, not a loving spirit. Laws are not made any less external for being weakened.

Nor is it even to be wished that they should be made any less external. Law and order is an entirely external state of affairs, but none the less desirable for that. If justice ceases to be objective it simply ceases to be justice. There may even be times when the Church itself is concerned, and honourably concerned, with the establishment or maintenance of justice, possibly as a necessary preliminary to preaching the Gospel. What matters is not that the Church should inevitably hold itself aloof from everything merely legal, but that if it does find itself concerned with legality it shall understand what it is doing and recognize two important logical consequences.

The first of these is that in so far as the Church deals with duty it cannot deny rights, which are the correlatives of duties. Justice in fact is a sort of two-edged weapon. On the one hand it shows people what they owe to others when they are not yet ready to love them; but on the other hand it simultaneously shows people their own rights which must be admitted to be equally real. Sometimes a whole society makes a moral advance : for example, looking after the weak becomes a duty where before it counted as an extra kindness; but the concept of duty and rights as correlative is not altered, for the weak then have a right to be looked after. It is not possible to escape the conclusion that so long as we are thinking in terms of duty, however gently enforced, we cannot avoid thinking in terms of rights as well. If I have a duty to do so much, then I have a right to stop there. If you have a duty to do something for me, then I have a right that you should do it. To suggest that all duties apply to oneself and all rights to other people is a sort of 'jam yesterday, jam to-morrow, but never jam to-day.' Even if no punishments are proposed and conscience is the only sanction duty is still something external and limited. It is something we can do, know that we have done, and say that we have done. If any organization or community, whether Church, state, school, club or neighbourhood, tries to press the idea of duty too far it will simply come up against people's rights. If charity is insisted on in such a way as to seem to thwart justice, 'It's not fair' will be the most likely answer, and it will be a true answer. Even if there is no revolt, people will 'do their duty' in a detached or even a resentful spirit, satisfying conditions laid down rather than committing their lives. This is not just a regrettable practical difficulty : it is morally reasonable. Duty is a sort of

moral taxation, something demanded of one from outside. There is no
need to go out of one's way to exceed its demands.

These limitations do not invalidate the idea of duty, nor even suggest
that the Church should never pronounce upon it, so long as it understands that getting people to do their duty is a way of bringing about
certain outward results, not of getting them to love God and each
other. For example, if society is lawless, this is a bad state of affairs
in itself, and the Ten Commandments assume an importance which in
more peaceful times will be overlaid by specifically Christian teaching.
Again, if the Church needs money it may find it desirable to lay it down
as a duty that people shall give; but if it wants generosity it must try
some other method.

The point comes out particularly clearly over the question of church
attendance. It makes good sense for the Church to legislate, even for-
mally, about what services are to be held, who is responsible for holding
them, and who is to keep the church buildings in a fit state; for the aim
here is the external fact that certain services shall take place, in order
that people shall be able to go to them and worship God. It is much
more doubtful whether it is sensible for the Church to lay it down as
a duty that people shall go to the services, for the object is not the
external fact of attendance but the personal relationships with God
and each other of which public worship is intended to be an expression.
Reluctant or detached prayers are like reluctant or detached visits to
parents, with the difference that God will always know if His children
are only being polite. Filial duty misses the main point of filial love.

No doubt the question is more complicated. Certainly a tradition of
going to Church regularly is helpful, and the absence of such a tradition
at the present time is a great hindrance to many people. It is natural
to hope that obligatory churchgoing will form a good habit and even
that someone who finds himself unwillingly in Church will
be captivated or at least edified by what he discovers there. This may
happen; but it is just as probable that people who are made to go to
Church will look on it as an imposition and be alienated rather than
encouraged. It is not just a question of outward compulsion, rebellion
and punishment, but rather of dutiful churchgoing becoming a debt to
be paid, something one would happily be let off, a deduction from one's
Sunday freedom. This kind of conformity, however obedient, is emphati-
cally not a good second best to the Psalmist's gladness at going to the
house of the Lord [2]; and nor does mechanical churchgoing set a par-

[2] Psalm 122: 1.

ticularly good example to other people. If people need guidance about going to Church, as for instance confirmation candidates may wonder how often to go to Communion at first, it is suitable and desirable for the Church to give it, but recommendations are a different sort of thing from regulations. To put the matter another way, inadequate churchgoing is a symptom not a disease, and to treat a symptom on its own is as dangerous as to ignore a symptom.

The Church need never deny that outward results are important, and it need not always refuse to be concerned with them. For a Church to take a hand in government or for it to make pronouncements about public affairs is not necessarily to confuse the legal with the personal, so long as it knows what it is doing and fully understands that if it enters the political field it must be prepared to be judged in political terms. Nor is it necessarily an illegitimate interference for the Church to be concerned with the affairs of this world. The spiritual and the temporal cannot be rigidly distinguished and if God is concerned with the whole of men's lives so may His Church be. If temporal conditions are such that men are living like beasts the Church ought to say so and do all it can to help. This kind of concern will often express itself in charitable works, but sometimes it will require political activity. There is of course a need for caution here : for the Church to commit political errors may be a way of taking the Name of the Lord in vain.

But justice and political wisdom are not enough. The second essential principle for the Church to remember is that its legal and political activities, however admirable, leave its positive task not yet begun and perhaps even endangered. In so far as it becomes either a legal system or a political power it becomes unlike the family, not by being larger or more highly organized, not by being disciplinary, but by losing its primary concern with personal relationships. It is then rather as if Christian people were children in a school run by their own parents, whom they hardly ever saw except in their capacity as teachers. If the school were badly or tyrannically run the situation would be disastrous and the children would be getting stones instead of bread; but even if the school were excellent as a school something essential would be lacking.

It is easy enough to say that the spirit of love is the main concern of the Church and that unless it is to be content with merely outward results it must somehow help people to go beyond duty; it is very much more difficult to see how this is to be put into practice. To say, 'Yes, indeed, the Church must teach that more is required of us than just our duty' is to fall into a logical trap. If something is 'required' of us it simply is our duty, or else it is an unfair demand, and in neither case is duty transcended. This difficulty is bound to arise as long as the Church thinks of its distinctive moral message in terms of duty at all. What it needs is a completely different starting point.

To say however that the Church must concern itself instead with personal relationships in order to achieve the spirit of love sounds like a platitude. To be any use it needs to be given some positive content. This is where the family analogy is useful, for it shows what is wrong with the prevalent picture of religion as primarily a matter of being good. It would never occur to a normal human father on being asked what he most wanted for his children to reply, 'That they should be good.' He would be much more likely to say that he wanted them above all to grow up into happy human beings. Of course he does want them to be good, but only because he believes that in the long run they cannot otherwise be happy. If we take the Fatherhood of God seriously it surely follows that what God most wants for His children is their eternal happiness, not in any superficial sense but in the words of the Epistle to the Ephesians, that they should all attain 'to mature manhood, measured by nothing less than the full stature of Christ.' [3] If the Church can teach this doctrine of God with conviction the whole of Christian morality falls into place. It ceases to be a matter of requirements but becomes one of loving relationships. To be a good Christian is to bring forth the 'fruit of the Spirit,' [4] not to satisfy certain conditions.

It might be thought that this primary concern of the Church with personal relations would mean a selfish concentration upon its own affairs. An ordinary family cannot devote its entire time and attention to fostering its own family life. Certainly a Church which was exclusively occupied with trying to save the souls of its own members without regard for those outside would be an unedifying and unchristian spectacle; but then nor could one say that such a Church was really fostering the Christian family life. The real Christian life includes an active concern with the outer world, not incidentally nor occasionally but essentially, and for the Church to devote itself to its own proper affairs in this sense is certainly not selfish.

It seems at first sight as if we have now reached a genuine and

[3] Ephesians 4: 13 (New English Bible).
[4] Galatians 5: 22.

important difference between the Church and the family, for nothing in ordinary family life appears quite to correspond to the Church's task of preaching the Gospel to those outside. It is not just a matter of ordinary family loyalty, of maintaining the Church's integrity or of taking its part against attack : it is a positive, almost an aggressive function. Christians are not only the children of God, they are also His witnesses.

However it is not fanciful to remember at this point that any family will die out unless it continues to grow. The human family brings in new people, by marriage and sometimes by adoption, and it starts new lives by birth; and these are basic not incidental activities. To preach the Gospel is for the Church what 'to be fruitful and multiply and replenish the earth' is for the family.

This line of thought leads straight to a familiar piece of theology, that Baptism, the way we enter the Church, is a supernatural birth. In some ways this is a very difficult doctrine, but one aspect of it at least ought to be quite clear, that joining the Church is much more like joining a family than joining a club. It does not make very good sense to try to combine the idea of rebirth with theories about conditions of membership, rules and regulations, or legal status. It fits much better with such ideas as family affection, family traditions and family discipline.

Almost every one would agree that this way of thinking is the ideal basis for the life of the Church, and even that at its best the Church does achieve it, but the question is whether the ideal is so often likely to prove impracticable that it is foolish to adopt it as the only valid theory of the Church. Family discipline is the crux. If the Church is in any degree the Christian community under the guidance of the Holy Spirit family affection and family tradition are bound to grow; but some discipline will still be necessary, and once this discipline becomes at all elaborate it will not look very different from legal discipline merely because it is given a different label. It is extraordinarily difficult for the Church to take up any definite position about moral questions without becoming legalistic in practice. However hard it tries to treat people as individuals some kind of policy is needed if decisions are not to be arbitrary, and this can easily harden into a system of case law. Yet if on the other hand it refuses to take up any definite position Christian witness seems bound to be weakened.

The difficulty is a practical one and can only be solved in practice.

It is a matter of what the Church does in detail and of how well it succeeds in making its actions understood; but there are still certain considerations which may be put forward in the hope of making the practical solution more likely to be achieved.

In the first place, it matters enormously that the problem should be recognized as a problem. At present legalism is normally seen as a tolerable or even a good second-best to the family attitude. It needs to be reiterated that the results which law achieves are essentially outward results. This is still true even when the law is about supposedly spiritual or inward matters. It is a mistake to think that laws about people's private inner lives are any less legal than laws about their public outward actions. To overwork this distinction between the inner and the outer is harmful, not only because it suggests that we can take a unified human being to pieces, but also because it obscures the more important distinction between the legal and the personal. The nature of law is that it is imposed, and its results must therefore be external, whatever aspect of human nature they are concerned with. They may be excellent in their own way, but they are not even the beginning of the creation of loving personal relationships. If the Church recognizes this it can avoid walking into a sort of dead end.

But secondly, there is no need merely to affirm obstinately that the Church must not be legalistic. It is possible to give a little more idea of how it need not. In many moral difficulties we can only speculate about what Christ himself would have done, but here we have some definite Biblical guidance. Christ not only told us, presumably as individuals, not to judge other people; he himself refused to judge, and here his Church can surely take him as a model. For example, when someone asked him to adjudicate in a dispute over inheritance, 'he replied, "My good man, who set me over you to judge or arbitrate?"' [5] and when the Pharisees brought to him a woman caught in the act of adultery he was not willing to condemn her.[6] What is significant about both these stories is that we certainly do not interpret them either as diminishing Christ's authority or as suggesting that he condoned sin. The reason is that we are so sure on other grounds of his authority and his attitude to sin that we feel no perplexity. He can afford to refuse to give a legal judgment, because his real teaching is positive and personal. In the same way the Church can say, 'If law is

[5] Luke 12: 13–15 (New English Bible).
[6] John 8: 1–11.

E

what you want, go to a lawyer,' or even 'Neither do we condemn you,' provided that this is firmly founded on a basis of constructive teaching about what Christian love really is. This is not a way of evading the problem, but is rather the only way of facing it. The problem of church discipline will always be insoluble as long as it is treated on its own. The Church will not succeed in making people Christian by imposing fragments of the Christian Way upon them, but only by presenting the Christian Gospel as a whole and letting it be seen as something both real and profoundly desirable.

CHAPTER 8

An illustration: the problem of Divorce

THE only way to show that the views I am putting forward are not vague idealism is to give a practical example in some detail. The problem of what the Church's attitude should be towards divorce and remarriage presents itself here with considerable urgency. It is a matter of first-class importance both to Christians and non-Christians, where the teaching of the Church is clearly seen to impinge upon people's lives, and where the interpretation of the New Testament pronouncements, definite though they seem to be, is by no means straightforward. When it comes to applying the Christian doctrine of marriage to modern life people of goodwill find themselves taking up profoundly opposed positions.

There are three main views on divorce and remarriage current in the Church of England to-day. Each of them is supported by weighty arguments, but none of them is ultimately satisfactory. The first is the Rigorist view, which is the same as that held in the Church of Rome. Rigorists maintain that divorce is in fact impossible and that those who remarry afterwards are actually living in sin, so that however hard the case nothing can be done for them unless they will give it up. The second is the view of those who emphasize that Christ did not legislate and that the Church is concerned with individuals : it may therefore be called the Pastoral view. It is persuasively set out in the pamphlet [1] by the Provost of Sheffield and Canon Bryan Green to which I have already referred.[2] They maintain that divorce is not impossible but wrong, and that a second marriage, if based on penitence for the failure of the first, can be built up into a true Christian marriage. The third is the view that the Church ought to recognize that there are two standards of marriage, legislate strictly for its own members, and give up the attempt to force its rules on those outside.

This 'Two Standards' view is the most convincing at first sight, simply because in a partially Christian society it is bound to appear to fit best with the facts. On the one hand there are Christian marriages which

---

[1] *Marriage, Divorce and Repentance in the Church of England.*
[2] See above, p. 26.

put into practice the Christian ideal, and on the other hand there are marriages over which the Church has no control at all; and it seems only common sense to urge the Church to recognize this and confine the idea of indissolubility to marriages which are explicitly Christian. This might seem to be a good way of reconciling the other two opposing views; but on consideration it cannot be acceptable to either. What it really means is that one should be Rigorist about those who have been married in Church and ignore the rest. The theory is therefore a form of Rigorism, and from a Pastoral point of view it will be open to many of the objections which can be made to Rigorism : these cannot all be answered by merely limiting its scope.

Nor is the 'Two Standards' view any more acceptable to Rigorists than to those who dislike Rigorism. They can attack it on both theoretical and practical grounds. For example, the Bishop of Exeter insists that since the priest and the registrar are 'only witnesses,' 'a marriage in a registry office is just as much a marriage . . . as a marriage in Church'[3]; and that indissolubility 'is right and God's will for every marriage, not just Christian marriages.'[4] This is not just the Church refusing to relinquish any authority : Christ's teaching about marriage points back before Christianity, before Moses, to the creation of men and women,[5] and to explain it as a special law for Christians is to deny it. Moreover in practice to recognize two standards of marriage would be bound to mean that people on the fringes of the Church would be driven out and a fine opportunity for evangelizing would be lost. It is not only divorced people who come and ask for a Church wedding with very little idea of what Christianity is, and the Rigorist as much as anybody wants to teach these people and bring them into the flock, not to lose all touch with them from the very outset.[6]

If we therefore abandon the Two Standards theory we are left with the other two, each of which would claim to be the more 'Christian.' The Pastoral view certainly has much to commend it to those who emphasize the Church's duty 'to seek and to save the lost.'[7] It is deeply concerned about individual troubles, yet it is not entirely unmindful of the corporate aspect of the question.[8] The Provost of

---

[3] R. C. Mortimer, *Christian Ethics,* p. 112.
[4] R. C. Mortimer, *The Duties of a Churchman,* p. 10.
[5] Mark 10: 2–12. See Genesis 1: 27; 2: 24; 5: 2.
[6] cf. T. A. Lacey, *Marriage in Church and State,* ed. R. C. Mortimer, p. 189f.
[7] Luke 19: 10.
[8] See e.g. Cruse and Green, p. 41.

Sheffield and Canon Green stress that, far from weakening the Church's witness, pastoral care for the divorced on the lines they propose can even be a way of affirming the Christian doctrine of marriage and building up true Christian lives. To them it is the Rigorist attitude which is weakening the witness of the Church in the eyes of the world. 'It is not the case,' they urge,[9] 'that those outside are "offended" by the Church's strong stand, knowing in their hearts that the Church is right, but rather that they think the Church to be unchristian and unhelpful.'

This is at least partly true; but the dangers of obscuring the Christian doctrine of marriage remain. Some divorced people certainly feel at present, not that they must try to discover the Will of God for them, but that they must try to discover a clergyman whose views about divorce are not too strict. The idea is already very prevalent that divorce and remarriage are the natural remedy for marriage troubles. Of course people expect their own marriages to last, but if anyone is in difficulties they naturally tend to recommend the ordinary way out. If even the Church teaches that remarriage can be acceptable it is bound to encourage this kind of 'divorce-mindedness.'

But even if one could avoid these objections to the Pastoral view there remain two great difficulties for it. The first is that it is not comprehensive enough. Canon Green admits [10] that on this view there are 'a certain number of cases where it is impossible to go forward,' and where he can only offer 'a friendly understanding.' He mentions particularly 'those difficult moral cases' where the marriage of A and C is in question, and it turns out 'that the previous marriage of A and B was broken up entirely through A's meeting with and love for C.' But a very large number of marriages which finally break up do so because one partner wants to marry someone else; these are not a handful of special cases, and one cannot be sure that they are invariably the least deserving ones. If the Pastoral view has to exclude these it has failed on its own ground. It avoids Rigorism, but not legalism.

Secondly, and still more serious, one cannot in conscience deny that the Pastoral view has to give a forced interpretation of the teaching of Christ. It might indeed be said that it goes completely against it. The plausibility of the theory depends on the idea that in some cases divorce and remarriage are completely separate and that the sinfulness is attached to the divorce and not to the remarriage.[11] Just as the mur-

[9] p. 46.
[10] p. 49.
[11] e.g. Cruse and Green, p. 22.

derer has really killed his victim, and cannot bring him back even by repentance, so it is suggested that the divorced person has really killed his marriage, and is not committing a new sin by marrying again.

But the Gospels indicate nothing of the kind. On the contrary, 'whoever divorces his wife and marries another, commits adultery against her.' [12] The Gospel according to St. Matthew adds, 'and whoever marries a divorced woman commits adultery.' [13] This comparison of remarriage after divorce to adultery [14] is as well-authenticated and explicit as anything in the Gospels.[15] Nor is it out of keeping with the rest of Christ's teaching. His notable power to understand individual cases did not come from a mild tolerance which tells people to please themselves, but from an authoritative but forgiving love which tells them to 'sin no more.' [16] Attempts to explain away his pronouncements on divorce can only sound like specious casuistry to a Rigorist, however much he may respect the motive of Christian charity which actuates them. The teaching was felt to be hard at the time [17] : we have no right to try to wriggle round it.

The Rigorist view, on the other hand, has the great advantage of endeavouring to hold fast the plain meaning of Christ's words. Those who hold it are willing to accept unpalatable logical consequences. They will not compromise Christian principles by allowing people to eat their cake and have it, or weaken their witness to the sanctity of Christian marriage by making exceptions for hard cases. There is always forgiveness, they would say, for the worst of sinners, but to be forgiven people must repent, and one cannot, as Shakespeare's Claudius sees, 'be pardoned and retain the offence.' Some of the cases are very hard, but all the Church can do is to try to help people to repent : it cannot

[12] Mark 10: 11.
[13] Matthew 5: 32.
[14] The interpretation of the Matthæan qualification (5: 32; 19: 9) 'except on the ground of unchastity' is a complicated question, but I am accepting the arguments of many scholars (e.g. Dewar *An Outline of New Testament Ethics,* pp. 94–5) that it was not part of what the Lord actually said. This means that St. Mark's Gospel, the older, is also the truer account. It is surely much the easier to believe. To allow divorce for adultery but for no other cause creates far more problems than it solves, whether on a Rigorist or a Pastoral view of Christ's teaching. I am inclined to interpret the addition as either an early relaxation of the stringency of Christ's command, the Church like Moses being faced with the hardness of people's hearts, or else as an attempt to allow for certain kinds of nullity. It is noteworthy that the word translated 'unchastity' does not normally mean 'adultery.'
[15] See above, pp. 16f., 26f.
[16] John 8: 11.
[17] Matthew 19: 10.

say that they may go on living in sin without repentance. If there is really no such thing as divorce, to marry somebody, whether innocent or guilty, who has a previous partner living is to go through a form of marriage only : it is unthinkable for the Church to countenance this in any way, however harsh the consequences may be in practice.

This is a point of view which one must respect. The trouble is that the hardness of some of the cases is of a peculiar kind. Claudius found repentance too difficult for him : 'Yet what can it when one can not repent?' Many divorced people are faced by an even worse question, 'What can it' when one *may* not repent, when to repent in the sense required of them would only make matters worse. Perhaps their first marriage is broken beyond repair, whereas by marrying again, how-ever wrongly, they have taken on real responsibilities to other people, especially if they have had children by the second marriage. It is neither practical nor Christian to say that they ought to abandon these responsibilities, nor to say that they must pay the price by being per-manently cut off from the Church. There is something wrong with a doctrine which leaves no way of repentance open to people who want to do their duty. Nor is it any better for people in this predicament to undertake to 'live as brother and sister' ; this is only a more subtle way of abandoning responsibilities and breaking more vows. In par-ticular, it is not a way of doing their duty by their children while keeping themselves free from sin : children ought to grow up in a real family life, not a sham one full of unnatural tension.

But what makes the Rigorist view even harder to maintain is that the decision in some of the hard cases seems to depend not on any moral situation but on luck. The Provost of Sheffield quotes the case [18] of a divorced man who was later converted to Christianity and 'was given permission . . . to be married again in Church, on the grounds of Pauline privilege.[19] This was given because as a baby he had not been baptized. If he had, the permission would not have been given.' Or one might put the case of a man who has married a divorced woman. Rigorists would say that he is really living in sin, committing adultery with a married woman. If this 'marriage' breaks up, perhaps because the man finds someone he likes better, they must surely allow that he is free to marry again, however solemnly he made vows to his first 'wife' and however long they were established as a married

[18] p. 34.
[19] See below, p. 75, note 25.

couple. He is better able to present himself at Communion with his new wife than when he was being faithful to his first vows. Worse still, he is better able to present himself at Communion than an ex-wife who has been cruelly treated or deserted by an entirely unsatisfactory husband and who after many years has found somebody to look after her.

It is small wonder that at this point people begin to say, 'If this is the Christian doctrine of marriage, so much the worse for Christianity. It is not moral, it is unfair.' Now this has a very familiar sound : we have seen already that Christianity is not 'fair.' [20] Just as human love asks more of us than can 'reasonably' be expected, so does the teaching of Christ. It cannot therefore be enforced as law, or injustice will be the only result. It can only be kept if law is transcended and the spirit of love is achieved, and to this there is no legal or even dutiful short-cut. There is no reason to suppose that Christ's teaching on divorce is an exception to this. It is most significant that one of the contexts in which it appears in the Gospels is the 'Sermon on the Mount,' where it is placed in a series of new commandments in which we are told to act in a different spirit from the old Law.[21] There is no suggestion that the commandment on divorce is on a different footing from the commandments on murder or lust : 'You have learned that our forefathers were told, "Do not commit murder; anyone who commits murder must be brought to judgment." But what I tell you is this : Anyone who nurses anger against his brother must be brought to judgment . . . You have learned that they were told, "Do not commit adultery." But what I tell you is this : If a man looks on a woman with a lustful eye, he has already committed adultery with her in his heart.' Only two verses separate this commandment on lust from the parallel commandment on divorce : 'They were told, "A man who divorces his wife must give her a note of dismissal." But what I tell you is this : If a man divorces his wife for any cause other than unchastity [22] he involves her in adultery; and any one who marries a woman so divorced commits adultery.' Again only a few verses separate this from the command, 'If a man wants to sue you for your shirt, let him have your coat as well.' All this suggests very strongly that whatever interpretation we give to Christ's teaching on divorce must also be capable of covering his teaching on anger, lust and going to law.

[20] See above, p. 29.
[21] Matthew 5 : 21–48 (New English Bible).
[22] See above, p. 70, note 14.

This may help us, most certainly not to water down his principles, but to see their real significance. From a Christian point of view, he who hates his brother is a murderer; and likewise he who puts away his wife and marries another is an adulterer. We do not expect the Church to try to tighten up the law of murder to cover those who hate, and nor should it try to insist on a strict law of marriage which would make it impossible to seek redress for genuine wrongs. This does not mean that the Church gives permission for Christians to divorce, any more than it gives them permission to hate. It should not pronounce favourably or unfavourably upon a man's rights, but say 'Never mind your rights. Here is a better way altogether.'

If someone comes and asks, 'May I as a Christian remarry after divorce?' he is like a man who asks, 'May I as a Christian claim damages in a law court for a wrong that has been done to me?' or 'May I as a Christian kill someone in self-defence?' The answer is : You have the right. Your action will not be invalid or even immoral. But you cannot say you are doing it 'as a Christian.' To some extent, possibly very slight but possibly very great, to claim one's rights is to betray the Christian spirit by returning to the hardness of heart which needs law. There is no *Christian* answer to the question, 'In what circumstances may I divorce my wife?' any more than there is to the question, 'How little need I give to the poor?' or 'How often must I forgive my brother?' To answer questions like this is for the lawyer or the moralist : if the Church attempts it it has inevitably stepped outside the Christian family spirit.

Here the objection arises that the Church is simply not able in practice to dissociate itself in this way from legal problems. From its very beginning it has been not only tempted but often obliged to legislate, and in particular the law of marriage and divorce has always been one of its special concerns. It is unrealistic to brush all this aside or even entirely to deplore it, but it need not be fatal to the present theory. When by force of circumstances the Church has to be a legal entity there is always the *danger* of legalism swamping its family life; but dangers can sometimes be overcome. The existence of the danger certainly does not prove the non-existence of the family life.

In fact at present in this country the Church is particularly favourably placed for keeping itself clear of legal problems. We have a respected and well-intentioned State, secular without being anti-clerical, which makes and administers laws which are very widely agreed to be basically just and reasonable. Just as the efficient maintenance of law and order sets the Church free to preach the doctrine of Christian love, so the fact that the law of divorce has been taken out of the Church's hands makes the Church more free, not less, to preach its positive doctrine of Christian marriage.[23]

It is true on the other hand that whatever the legal and social system the Church will still sometimes have to pronounce on legal questions. It may be imperative to declare explicitly whether a man has ever been married before or not, for if a marriage has never existed there can be no reason whatever to refuse a wedding in church. This means that the Church cannot refuse to give legal decisions about annulments, but no harm need be done so long as it knows what it is doing. Decisions of this kind are definite legal decisions on the same level as those given in the Courts, which can plainly be seen to be law rather than Gospel. What the Church should avoid is the attempt in the name of the Gospel to give new pseudo-legal decisions, at what is meant to be a higher and more Christian level, about questions which already have legal answers. This is the way to create hard cases and bad law, not to build up Christian lives.

For a man who has once been married to make up his mind that although he is free to marry again according to law and common-sense morality, he is not free personally and in the sight of God, is an intensely difficult decision which in the last resort he must make for himself. His Church may be able to help him to decide, but only as parents can help a grown-up child, by individual advice and sympathy. To try to fit his case into a system and govern him by a rule may seem easier but it is not a help, for he is already beyond the stage of rules. The danger is not that he will be immoral but that he will be unfaithful, and faith is a relation between persons, not a subject for legislation.[24] If he is already pledged for life to another woman, however unworthy she may have turned out to be, he cannot in honour make these vows again, and if he knows what God's standard of marriage is he cannot in honour do anything to destroy that standard in the eyes of the world. If he has never really been pledged although he has been legally married before beginning to be a Christian, it is just conceivable that he may be in all honesty a free man. This could be

---

[23] See above, p. 66.
[24] The Provost of Sheffield distinguishes adultery as lust and adultery as unfaithfulness (pp. 21–2), but uses the distinction rather differently.

used as a way of understanding the 'Pauline privilege' that a Christian is not bound to an unbeliever who has departed [25]; but in our society, where the distinction between believer and unbeliever is far from clear-cut, it would be very difficult to make much use of it without becoming enmeshed in legalism again. What needs above all to be emphasized is that this kind of problem is a matter of personal relationships, which it is a perilous matter for any one outside to attempt to judge.

At this point a strange inconsistency seems to appear and needs to be explained. I have suggested that while not judging other people the Christian will always tend as a matter of personal loyalty to reject remarriage after divorce for himself; whereas in considering the equally thorny question of pacifism he will assess the situation on its merits and may decide on actions which apparently disobey Christ's commands.[26] Here a distinction needs to be drawn. In the first place, Christ's commands about both violence and divorce ask more of us than can 'fairly' be expected and therefore ought not to be set up as objective moral laws : it is only 'in the spirit of love' that they can be kept. But in the second place, in the case of pacifism there are other relevant arguments besides the hardness of the hard cases and the reasonableness of people's rights. The pacifist has to consider whether by personally refraining from violence he is only leaving distasteful actions to be performed by somebody else; and whether perhaps he is even making himself responsible for violence that might have been avoided. The man who rejects divorce for himself is not making himself responsible for divorces, and cannot fairly be accused of leaving the remarrying to other people. His difficulty in applying Christ's teaching may be acute, but it is a different kind of difficulty from the pacifist's problem.

The chief advantage of the present way of looking at the question of divorce is not that people may be excused from acting in a Christian spirit but that they may start at any time. They are not beyond help, even if as a result of their past behaviour they are involved in a situa-

---

[25] I Cor. 7: 12–15: 'To the rest I say this, as my own word, not as the Lord's: if a Christian has a heathen wife, and she is willing to live with him, he must not divorce her; and a woman who has a heathen husband willing to live with her must not divorce her husband . . . If on the other hand the heathen partner wishes for a separation, let him have it. In such cases the Christian husband or wife is under no compulsion; but God's call is a call to live in peace' (New English Bible).
[26] See above, p. 51.

tion which they ought never to have been in, but from which they cannot now disentangle themselves without doing worse harm. Their actions have been unchristian, but valid. The man who has put away his wife and married again has insisted on his legal rights. This was a betrayal of the Christian spirit, and from the point of view of Christ's teaching he has committed adultery, but this does not mean that he is necessarily still in a quasi-legal state of 'living in sin,' any more than a man who has once brought a lawsuit against his enemies instead of forgiving them is considered to have stolen his own property because he did not make a present of it to his antagonists. The question of whether a man is living sinfully depends upon the spirit in which he is living now, not upon the spirit in which he has acted in the past, still less upon events beyond his control such as whether or not he was baptized as a baby. If he now repents of something he has once done he should make restitution if he can; but the possibility of repentance cannot depend upon the possibility of restitution.

If this argument is sound the problem of the admission of divorced people to Holy Communion is greatly eased. The Church of England certainly seems to be coming more and more to the conclusion that it is wrong and unchristian to refuse Communion as a penal measure. A Sacrament is a means of grace, not a good conduct prize or a health certificate, and nobody should think to come to it on a basis of merit. Moreover to make divorce a more serious bar to receiving Communion than, for example, sharp business dealings or uncharitableness is to run a grave risk of putting one's emphasis in moral teaching quite differently from where Christ placed it. Yet there are many who are still worried about applying this to divorced people who have re-married, for to take Communion in an unrepentant state is a sham and a sacrilege, and it seems a matter of plain logic that those who have remarried after divorce must inevitably be unrepentant sinners. Some Rigorists try to reconcile mercy and principle by suggesting that those who have remarried with good consciences in the sincere belief that they were not doing wrong should be allowed Communion; but this has the curious effect of making unrepentance a condition rather than repentance.

If the view which I am putting forward is correct one need not after all put the problem of divorce in a different category from other moral questions. A man who has remarried after divorce is like a man who has successfully sued his enemy for damages. The one has not necessarily been lustful in the ordinary sense any more than the other has necessarily been vindictive, but neither has acted in the Christian spirit.

It may be thought that remarriage cannot be compared with lawsuits in this way because divorce breaks marriage vows, but this is not an insuperable objection. Legally speaking, it is possible to be absolved from vows, even vows to God. If people can be released from convents so they can from marriages, so far as their legal and moral status is concerned. Whether or not they have broken their faith with God is for God only to judge; but to refuse them Communion is to deny them the ordinary means for sinners to approach God and restore broken faith.

To ask how soon after a deliberate second marriage the Church should encourage people to come back to Communion is like asking how soon after a legal action for damages it should encourage them to come. These questions are difficult precisely because they cannot be answered by rules. People's attitudes are so complex and diverse that they cannot be classified neatly into high-handed presumption, innocent good intentions, and sincere penitence, and to legislate is inevitably to falsify.

The question of remarriage in Church or services of blessing is altogether different. It is not legalism to say that the Church can hardly give its formal blessing to people when they are actually doing what Christ particularly wished them not to do.[27] No doubt it may be argued on behalf of services of blessing that it is a deep-seated human instinct to ask for God's blessing; that wherever possible this should be encouraged; that the Church is certainly right to try to bless people even when it cannot bless their actions; and that this should be carried very far for the sake of the pastoral good it does. The analogy of church parades may be urged; the cynical or the severe can say that they are a way of blessing violence, yet they also seem to be a way of helping to keep violence under control.

But in spite of this the arguments on the other side cannot be denied. These point out that it is a deep-seated human instinct to try to eat one's cake and have it, and that the Church is only weakening its witness if it gives any kind of solemn blessing to what Christ explicitly called adultery. The Church is not there to tell us to do just what we please, but to preach the Gospel.

The apparent harshness of this doctrine would be mitigated if two

[27] See above, p. 5of.

things were made clear. First, the Church should recognize, fully and not grudgingly, the validity of a civil marriage after a civil divorce, just as it recognizes the validity of a civil lawsuit to redress a wrong. Secondly, it should not regard a failure to uphold the Christian spirit in marriage as necessarily a ground for excommunication any more than, for instance, a failure to uphold the Christian spirit in trade. People often step outside the sphere of Christian love and claim their rights, and very often in doing this they betray the spirit of Christianity, but to be a sinner is not necessarily to be an 'open and notorious evil liver.' To distress one's family is not the same thing as to flout it or cut oneself off from it.

This theory about what the Church's attitude ought to be towards divorce and remarriage certainly does not abolish all difficulties; but the difficulties should now appear in the right place, where one would expect them. They will be difficulties of decision, not of interpretation. Instead of looking for loopholes in a law people are to ask what from now on they really ought to do. Presumably moral decisions will always be hard. A theory which made moral problems sound easy would be as suspect as one which made them insoluble. It should indeed be emphasized that sometimes acting in a Christian way will demand real heroism. People may find that they must be loyal to a marriage in which they are miserable with no real hope of better times, or that they must give up the society of another person with whom they are deeply in love. But they will be doing these things from a positive spirit of love, not because no way can be found of avoiding the application of a law. Christianity ought to be heroic; but it ought not to be unreasonable. It *is* unreasonable if people are obliged to cut themselves off permanently from the Sacraments for the sake of others to whom they have wrongly but really taken on responsibilities; or to condemn others who to all appearance are more sinned against than sinning; or on the other hand to try to twist the words Christ is reported to have said to try to make them sound more lenient. On the present view one may recognize the validity of the ordinary law of decent behaviour and yet understand how it ought to be transcended.

CHAPTER 9

Duty to God

I HAVE been maintaining on the one hand that the commands of Christ are not a new code of laws, and on the other hand that they are supposed to be kept and that the ordinary law of decent behaviour 'ought' to be transcended. This may sound like a notable example of the human instinct to try to eat one's cake and have it. To insist that although Christ did not 'legislate' we must still literally obey him seems to suggest a new legalism which has not even the merit of straight thinking. The problem of the Church's attitude to the divorce sayings has raised this difficulty quite sharply: further explanation is therefore needed.

I have already rejected the solution that Christ's commands are not to be taken literally but only express ideals and indicate the spirit in which we ought to act. It is not good enough to concede after all that Christians may simply use violence, go to law and remarry after divorce with a clear conscience provided that they can persuade themselves they are really acting 'in a spirit of love.' This phrase can cover almost anything short of positive and active spite. It is a way of making the Sermon on the Mount practically a dead letter.

On the other hand I have also rejected the Rigorist solution of treating Christ's precepts as straightforward commands which we are required to keep as laws. It is not just accidental that the only piece of characteristic Christian teaching we really feel able to insist on is the prohibition of active animosity. We recognize it as a 'fair' demand, whereas we know quite well in practice that by contrast most of Christ's teaching asks more than can 'reasonably' be expected.

Yet we are not willing to say that it need not be obeyed. I have tried to show that this dilemma cannot be resolved by impaling oneself bravely on either horn; but nor is it any use to attempt to evade it by wrapping the whole problem up in meaningless words. It remains to be seen whether the solution I have suggested is any more than an evasion of this kind.

What is necessary is to examine more closely the statement that the commands of Christ cannot be kept 'as laws.' If this were just a way

79

of trying to cover up the unpalatable fact that we look on them in practice as wholly unrealistic it would be better to say outright, 'They cannot be kept'; but I believe it is possible to give a more constructive account. The Christian Way is not impracticable, but it cannot be adopted piecemeal. We cannot successfully set about obeying Christ's particular commands directly as a set of rules for the good life, like a recipe for a pudding. It is as 'fruit of the Spirit' that they can be kept. There is a world of difference between the idea that 'in the spirit of love' we shall be able to live naturally according to Christ's commands, and the idea which is often substituted for it, that 'in the spirit of love' we may break his commands as we think fit.

Two questions arise immediately. The first and most pressing is, How can we achieve this 'spirit of love'? The second is, If the particular commands cannot be kept as such, why were they given? Both these questions can be answered by considering a little further what the Gospel consists of. Taken as a whole, it is the revelation of the love of God and at the same time it is the offer of a way of life, and these two aspects cannot be separated. The nearest human analogy is really a proposal of marriage. One knows that to accept it involves one's whole personality and one cannot expect to remain unchanged, but people who marry do not generally set out to alter themselves into something different by their own deliberate efforts. They simply grow differently, for better or worse, and as time goes on a characteristic family spirit emerges. In the same way becoming a Christian is a matter of accepting God's love, not of making oneself good by a conscious policy. Like marriage, Christian faith is not something we invent or a feeling we indulge in, nor is it merely a set of intellectual beliefs. To accept God's love with any sincerity is to begin to grow differently, and we are not left in doubt about how this will turn out in practice. The particular teaching in the Gospels is there to fill in the details. It shows the kind of people we shall become if we embark upon the Christian life.

But suppose that we do not embark upon the Christian life. Perhaps we would rather stand by our rights, keep the law, and refuse to transcend bare justice. Plenty of people do adopt this very attitude, and we cannot for ever evade the question of whether in the last resort it is a genuine alternative to acceptance of the Gospel. The analogy with marriage breaks down here, for marriage after all is a commitment which can be refused, but we dare not say that the Gospel is optional.

We surely cannot reply politely to God, 'No thank you, I would rather go my own way.' To make the difficulty still more acute, the commandment, 'Thou shalt *love* the Lord thy God' is not even part of the Gospel, it is part of the Law, and a part which Christ specifically endorsed.[1] We therefore seem bound to say that the love of God is compulsory, and if this is so it looks as if the whole interpretation of Christian morality as something which transcends plain justice is about to collapse. I have been maintaining that the Christian Gospel asks more than can 'fairly' be required of us, but now it appears that this is merely presumptuous. We are confronted by an absolute demand which leaves no room for any human rights, and when we have 'done all' we are still to say, 'We are unworthy servants; we have only done what was our duty.'[2]

The only way to deny that God's claim is indeed absolute is to deny that there is a God, and a Christian will be inclined to treat this as obvious; but he ought instead to face it as a difficulty. What it seems to imply is that in the last resort the idea of bare justice is a cheat. God is ready to give us much more than we can possibly deserve, but there is no real alternative to accepting His offer. Suppose like Shylock we do not ask for mercy but for justice we have no reason to suppose that the universe is as willing as the state of Venice to honour our bond.

The superficial answer is that we have no 'bond,' that legally we have not a leg to stand on and that to ask for justice is to ask for condemnation: but to think that this answer will satisfy is not to have grasped the problem. We did not ask to be created and we do not all ask for 'salvation.' The average man who is not specially interested in religion does not suppose that he deserves a heavenly prize, but to hope for a quiet life without suffering or interference does not seem unreasonable, and this is just what Christianity refuses to offer. To talk about divine judgment to someone who takes up this position is to present to him a God Who is not only legalistic but tyrannical. In affirming human unworthiness we must be very careful not to cast doubt on God's justice, or we shall find ourselves with a less worthy idea of Him than the old and crude assumption that some men really are innocent and can expect a righteous God to avenge their wrongs.[3]

The answer I would make is a tentative sketch rather than a com-

[1] Matthew 22: 37.
[2] Luke 17: 10.
[3] e.g. Psalm 64.

F

plete solution, but I think it represents the only way in which we can even begin to solve the problem. It is unhelpful to say 'Our rights do not matter because God will give us more than we deserve' or 'Our rights do not exist because we are all desperately wicked'; but it is more promising to say 'Our rights may be real but we cannot live on them.' In other words, plain justice is valid but it is not something which any one can really and ultimately want. A human personality is not a sort of hard and smooth little pellet which has no concern with others unless it is interfered with. On the contrary, it is something which grows by becoming engaged with the world about it and particularly with other personalities. To have wants, purposes, concerns and loves is not just a luxury, it is our nature. Detachment and neutrality are extremely sophisticated concepts, and if pushed to their limits are not only unusual but inhuman. To say that love is compulsory, therefore, is rather like saying that food is compulsory: we shall starve without it. It is a natural not a legal requirement. The man who in the last resort remains completely disengaged and refuses to commit himself to anything or any one is a monster, not a human being. He is not exactly forbidden to go his own way, but he has no way to go.

But once we let our personalities become engaged in any way whatever we are not independent of God. God is not one alternative commitment among many but in some way the basis of them all. This may sound like a piece of needless mystification if it is expressed philosophically as the 'immanence' of God, or even theologically as His dwelling in us and we in Him; but there is one place where it is expressed both simply and authoritatively, and carries immense conviction: 'Truly, I say to you, as you did it to one of the least of these my brethren, you did it to me,' and the converse, 'As you did it not to one of the least of these, you did it not to me.' [4] It is not only that God loves all His creatures and takes it as a personal offence if one of them is treated badly. It is not only that since He gave us all the loving relationships we have we owe Him a share in them. It is rather that the way we enter into relationships with the world about us will turn out in the end to have been, all along, the way we were actually entering into relationships with God. We cannot do nothing and be human; but whatever we do we are doing not only to each other but to God. This is not a difficult idea to see, although it is intensely

[4] Matthew 25: 40, 45.

difficult to give an explanation of it. It is certainly an integral part of
the Christian Gospel.

If this argument is sound we can still insist that the love of God is
a personal commitment not a legal claim, without having to draw the
corollary that it is an optional commitment we can decline. We are
all involved in God's love, whether we realize it yet or not, by the fact
of being human. Plain justice is not a cheat but an abstraction.

Nor does this way of approach in any way diminish the absoluteness
of God's claim : on the contrary. It is legal claims which are limited;
duties have rights as their correlatives [5]; but personal commitments
are in principle infinite. It is in this kind of context that it begins to be
natural, not appalling, to serve somebody without limit and still feel
one has done no more than one ought. The text about looking on
ourselves as unworthy servants is a particularly good example of a
commandment which makes nonsense as a piece of legislation but very
good sense as a description of Christian loyalty.

What is more important, the same may be said of the First Commandment itself. It is not part of the Gospel, it is part of the Law,
but the Jewish law is a special kind of law, full of foreshadowings of
the Gospel.[6] To treat it as purely 'legal' is the same kind of distortion
as it would be to treat the authority of parents over their immature
children as purely legal. The foundation of the Jewish religion is the
'Covenant' between the Lord and his people Israel, and the Covenant
is something much more personal than a sort of theocratic 'social con-
tract.' It is as much about love and faith as it is about duty and obligation. To talk about it in terms of duty is unsatisfactory because this way
of thinking is destructive of personal relationships. A detached husband
who does his duty to his wife or a detached mother who does her duty
to her children have not appreciated the real nature of the relationships
in which they are involved, and this is no less true of our relationships
with God.

But still we do want to talk about our duty to God, and not
entirely without good reason. If we abandon the stringency of the concept of 'duty' we tend to lose sight of the seriousness of what we owe
Him and of our own entire unworthiness to meet Him on equal terms.
The holiness of God is not something small and cosy which we can
take for granted, and His love is something of which we ought to be

---

[5] See above, p. 60.
[6] See above, p. 45.

in awe. In relation to it we simply are sinners. Indeed it is only at this stage in the argument that the concept of sin really makes sense. To talk legally about universal sinfulness is only to invite disbelief; but to present it as a failure to live up to God's love is to make it real and shameful. There is nothing abstract or merely theoretical about either the sin or the love : from this point of view the sin is a plain fact about human life, and the love is not something which we merely conjecture to make our picture of God complete but was shown in the most concrete way imaginable in Christ's death on the Cross. To say that God's claim upon us is personal not legal is not to belittle its absoluteness but to say that it is the claim of Someone Who loves us enough to die for us.

INDEX